W9-CNA-920

The Manley Art of Librarianship

Other Books by Will Manley

Snowballs in the Bookdrop
(1982)

Unintellectual Freedoms
(McFarland, 1991)

Unprofessional Behavior
(McFarland, 1992)

Unsolicited Advice
(McFarland, 1992)

For Library Directors Only
For Library Trustees Only
(McFarland, 1993)

Unsubstantiated Rumors
(McFarland, 1994)

The Manley Art of Librarianship

by Will Manley

Illustrations by Richard Lee

McFarland & Company, Inc., Publishers
Jefferson, North Carolina, and London

For my mother and father
on their fiftieth anniversary

British Library Cataloguing-in-Publication data are available

Library of Congress Cataloguing-in-Publication Data

Manley, Will, 1949–
    The Manley art of librarianship / by Will Manley.
        p.   cm.
    Includes bibliographical references (p.   ) and index.
    ISBN 0-89950-866-9 (lib. bdg. : 50# alk. paper)   ∞
    1. Library science – United States – Humor.   I. Title.
Z665.2.U6M36   1993
020'.973 – dc20   92-56664
                                                          CIP

Manufactured in the United States of America

McFarland & Company, Inc., Publishers
    Box 611, Jefferson, North Carolina 28640

CONTENTS

INTRODUCTION

Maybe this wasn't such a hot idea.

The knock on me over the years is that when I sit down at the word processor to write about librarianship I don't do my research, that I fly too much by the seat of my pants, and quite frankly that I don't know what I'm talking about. Actually I was once introduced that way before a keynote speech that I gave at a national bookmobile conference. The man who introduced me, a very earnest state librarian who I think really believed that he was paying me a big compliment, said, "And now please join me in giving a warm welcome to our guest speaker, Will Manley, the man who writes better about things he knows nothing about than anyone in the library profession."

At first I was a little taken aback, but then when I heard all the applause that followed I thought what the hey, at least I do something well. And then I launched enthusiastically and authoritatively into my views on bookmobile librarianship, a subject I know nothing about. Actually that's not quite true. I once totaled a bookmobile. No, that's not entirely true either. I really only "halved" it.

And then the person who was covering the bookmobile conference for the *Wilson Library Bulletin* critiqued my speech this way: "an inexcusably shallow presentation full of misinformation about bookmobiles."[1] I felt kind of bad about this critique until I realized that it had run in the September 1992 issue, which was the first issue of the magazine that had come out since I had been fired by Wilson's top brass from my twelve year stint as a monthly columnist. So I figured the dumpy review was a parting shot from them. Good riddance, Will.

The irony of my getting canned from Wilson was that the thing I got fired for, writing about librarians and sex, is actually something I do know something about. At least I know as much about it as any other librarian who has been married for twenty-three years and has three kids. Just my luck that the top brass at Wilson thought that the subject of sex was inappropriate to mix with the subject of librarians—kind of like vaseline and water in their mind. We librarians don't have sex, do we? Of course not. So where do librarians' babies come from? Here are some theories:

1. Test tubes
2. The stork
3. Outer space
4. Dr. Deweystein's workshop
5. Immaculate conceptions
6. The land of Oz

7. The Audioanimatronics Division of Disney
8. Christmas stockings
9. Surrogate parents
10. The Dismal Swamp in Georgia
11. The Tokyo Toyota factory
12. Chocolate Chip Cookie Dough
13. The Bionics Department of M.I.T.
14. The Muppet Workshop
15. The Original Cataloging Department of the Library of Congress

I had the last laugh on Wilson six months later. My vindication came along expeditiously, courtesy of my fellow author, Madonna, and the big controversy that she caused in Libraryland with her new book *Sex*. My question for the guys at Wilson is: If sex is not an appropriate subject for librarians to deal with, how come the library media's biggest story of 1992 focused on the issue of what librarians should do about Madonna's pictorial production?

Now, back to the subject of writing about things I know nothing about. That whole criticism of me actually didn't start with my introduction at the national bookmobile conference. To the best of my recollection it started with a bitingly critical editorial that John Berry wrote about me in *Library Journal* entitled "Facing the Cheap Shot."[2] What did I do to get Mr. Berry so bent out of shape? I had the temerity in one of my Facing the Public columns to question the importance of L.S.C.A. In John's eyes this was professional heresy. Since John doesn't have the power to excommunicate wayward librarians who violate our profession's code of political correctness, he did the next best thing — he excoriated me for writing "a poorly researched, two page cheap shot" and implied that I hadn't done my homework.

Actually, John and I are friends (at least I think we are), and I have a great deal of respect for him. I also owe a great deal to him for two reasons: (1) the editorial he wrote lambasting Wilson for firing me and (2) the editorial he wrote lambasting me for lambasting L.S.C.A. That's right, his "Facing the Cheap Shot" editorial actually put me on the map in the library profession. People wanted to know more about the guy who had been so successful in burning Berry's bacon.

Unfortunately, though, John's criticism has sort of stuck over the years like that stuff that collects in the cuffs of your pants. The twelve years of columns that I produced for Wilson produced a lot of mail, much of which was not very flattering except that most of the letter writers did manage to spell my name correctly. For some reason, people have the greatest temptation to leave the second "l" off of Will and the "e" off of Manley. Other than getting that right the nicest thing I could say about some of those letters was that they weren't attached to any explosive devices. They did have a common thread, however, in that they all thought I didn't know what I was talking about, which has always sort of bothered me even though I wouldn't admit it publicly.

So that's why I've written this book, and that's why this book is quite different from others that I've written. You won't find any of my quaint "I didn't get the job that I had desperately hoped for but the guy who did get it choked on a piece of pork and died and so the library board called me up and offered me the job so don't try to tell me that there's not a divine plan to the universe" type of story. No, this one is serious.

This time the homework I do will show. Flip quickly through the book. You couldn't help but notice that there are one hundred and eighty-nine works cited — not a world's record for a book of this size but certainly a big departure for me. A hundred and eighty-nine works cited — do you know how much research that represents? Let's just say that the librarians at the University of Arizona Library School library are greatly relieved that they'll never again have to fetch another dusty old trade journal or library treatise for moi. All their hard work was worth it, though, because the result is a book whose points are all anchored with the weight of scholarly authority.

As you flip through the book you'll notice that the scholarly works that I referred to are noted and collected at the end of each chapter. I chose this method of "endnoting" rather than "footnoting" because, although footnotes have the advantage of being more immediate to the reader, this immediacy can be distracting. It is my rather strong feeling that footnotes are indeed like the shoes on our feet. They have a definite purpose to serve but they are a complementary part of our wardrobe, not the main attraction.

As an author, therefore, I don't want my readers becoming so immersed in my bibliographical notes that they miss the actual points I am trying to make. I am in no way implying, please note, that we librarians are petty because of our proclivity to preoccupation with footnotes. I realize that this stems not from any character flaw but from the occupational habits that accrue from dealing with the minutiae involved with tracking bibliographic data.

I want to make it clear that I also recognize that by opting to use endnotes I am contributing to the decline and inevitable demise of the footnote as a literary accoutrement. A whole generation of students is growing up without exposure to the footnote. Those of us who labored on research papers and term papers in high school and college during the 50s and 60s remember the rigorous challenges that footnotes often presented. A proper footnote had to be exact, concise, and above all accurate. We can all remember with terror those teachers who were sadistic enough to check (or at least threaten to check) the veracity of a random sampling of our footnotes.

I still remember the compassion that I felt for a fellow history student in college who flunked a course on the New England colonies after having been caught red handed with four bogus footnotes on a paper he wrote on the topic of religious freedom at Plymouth Rock. Actually it was one of the best student papers that I have ever read, and certainly the lack of authenticity of those footnotes did nothing to diminish the excellence of the paper. Was it my friend's fault that the paper reflected his own original thinking and was not simply an unimaginative rehash of the ideas of others and that, therefore, he was forced to invent those footnotes in order to meet the overly pedantic requirements of our teacher? Finally, consider this: The format of those bogus footnotes was completely correct. They were concise without being spare and informative without being chatty. I always felt he deserved at least a "C" for creativity.

I think another professor of mine, a professor of English literature, would have agreed with me. He felt that the footnote had so much more potential than to serve as a mere vessel to convey bibliographical data. Properly done and with patience, he believed that the art of footnotery could lend a bit of literary quality to a piece of research or scholarship. By making subtle references to the value of the source it cites and by suggesting how that source fits into the literature of the field of knowledge to which it belongs, the footnote could serve as the missing ingredient needed to transform a piece of research into a work of literature.

But, according to my professor, footnoting is tricky business. While there is an understated eloquence to the deftly created footnote, the poorly prepared one can weight down the main text like barnacles encrusted on the bottom of a ship. That, I suppose, is why I've shied away from using footnotes here. In truth, my skill at the art of footnotery in college was rather dismal, and I have no reason to believe that the passing of twenty years has done anything to change things in that regard. We will, therefore, have to settle for the mediocrity of my end notes, taking comfort in the fact that at least they will not interfere with the text. The ultimate value of this publication will, therefore, neither be falsely elevated nor unfairly downgraded by the presence of footnotes.

If the art of footnotery is something that I have not engaged in for over two decades, the same cannot be said of the art of librarianship. For twenty-two years now, I have tinkered around in the library trade. Not only have I managed to make a living at it but I've also had what bankers, lawyers, ditch diggers, and the top management at the Wilson Company would probably consider to be an unfair amount of fun in the process. If life is not for fun, I ask you, what is it for?

I've had so much fun that I was tempted to title this book *The Joy of Librarianship* but thought better of it when I realized that fun and joy are two completely different things. Fun is a moment by moment kind of thing. It is having a patron ask you for the Blue Book price of a 1988 Chevy Corsica hatchback without the hatch. Joy, on the other hand, is something more permanent. It has more of an inner serenity quality to it even to the point of bordering on cosmic enlightenment. To me fun sounds a lot more fun than joy. Joy would be, therefore, much better suited for the title of a book on footnoting.

Actually the arts of librarianship and footnotery do have something in common — both are on the wane. Libraries are being replaced gradually by information centers, multimedia centers, and learning materials centers. In our era of super computers, mini computers, home computers, personal computers, lap-top computers, 180 cable television channels, a video rental store on every street corner, and a video game system in every home, the term "library" with its connotation of, God forbid should I say it, *books* just doesn't seem to suffice anymore. It is interesting to note, however, that as this movement toward the high tech has developed, there has been an accompanying movement — the downward trend of literacy rates, SAT scores, and standardized testing results in the lower grades.

It is important for me to emphasize, therefore, right from the beginning that this book celebrates the old fashioned art of librarianship with all of its idiosyncrasies. What is librarianship, you ask. I define it unapologetically as the process of bringing books and people together. Librarianship, contrary to all its old stereotypes, is essentially a people business, and librarians are people persons.

That, of course, is where the fun lies. Our patrons can be wonderful, sincere, grateful, creative, interesting, and even quite fascinating but they can also be stubborn, unruly, intimidating, obscene, and even violent. This is obviously, therefore, not a profession for the meek or humble. It is more for the manly and womanly among us. Chutzpah is a necessary prerequisite.

Is that why I've called this book the "Manley" Art of Librarianship? Yes, partly, but you'll also note that this "manley" is personalized with an "e." Above all, librarianship is a personalized profession. There are no hard and fast rules to it. Librarianship, unlike biology and chemistry, is not an academic discipline with an inherent body of knowledge. It is an art, not a science, and those of us who practice it are not androids in white lab coats. We are artists relying on our experience, our intuition, and our creativity. We make it up as we go along. It's a day to day, hour to hour proposition. We each have our own styles and philosophies. And so the word "Manley" in the title takes on a second meaning.

Finally, there is one last point to explain. I've used a self-questioning technique. Why? Am I attempting to be Socratic? No. The truth is that it was easier to write it that way. It allowed me to carve up a big subject into a lot of little chunks. I figure it will also be more convenient for you to read it that way (easier to skip the boring parts).

P.S. This book is somewhat organic in that it has an appendix. After you read the book you should remove the appendix (or photocopy it), fill it out honestly, and send it to me. As a magazine columnist used to getting a lot of mail (pro and con but mostly con), the most frustrating part of writing a book is the lack of response that you get from your readers, which assumes that somebody is actually going to read this through to the appendix, which come to think of it may be exactly the point.

P.P.S. If you don't want to fill out the survey in the appendix, then call me. I can be reached most weekdays at 602-350-5305 between 8 AM and 5 PM MST. I put this invitation in a previous book and a number of people did call me. It was great fun. Don't be shy.

Notes

1. Andros, Peter, "The Crash of the Public's Bookmobile," *Wilson Library Bulletin* (September 1992) 48–49. The accuracy of this article was challenged by a rebuttal article, "He Just Didn't Get It! What Really Happened at the Seventh Bookmobile Conference," which appeared on page 70 of the December 1992 *Wilson Library Bulletin*. It was written by Bill Crowley, deputy Ohio state librarian. Crowley is the person who put together the bookmobile conference. According to him, "both Jeffrey Krull [another conference speaker] and Will Manley did exactly as requested. These experienced, honorable gentlemen conscientiously addressed potentially hostile audiences to explain why bookmobile service was not a priority in their libraries. Andros's direct characterizations of Krull and Manley and his placement of a discussion of unnamed 'villains in the erosion of library access' immediately after paragraphs on them reflect something less than an ethical approach to reporting."

2. John Berry, "Facing the Cheap Shot," *Library Journal* (June 1, 1985) 49.

BOOKS

Son, that's a book. It won't play in the VCR. You have to read it.

How important is the book collection to a public library?

Book collections are important because, well, it's fairly difficult to imagine a library without a book collection of some sort. From time to time of course, you will hear library architects make the case that libraries can actually be designed with a much greater "library sense" by omitting book collection areas. These architects feel that if you just leave some books lying around on end tables and stairways that you can create a strong literary ambience without sacrificing the prime floor space that multiple ranges of shelving require. The principal proponent of the so-called "Zen school of library architecture" is I.M. Godbehare, who writes in his recent book *Zen Libraries and the Birds of Appetite* that what society really wants from its public libraries is "the concept of books, not the books themselves, and we should give them what they want."[1]

There are, of course, many spokespeople from the high tech world of electronic publishing who would argue that the book may soon become a modern day irrelevancy. Among them is Kulavian Messner who writes that our stubborn adherence to books and paper is just another manifestation of why we Americans are losing out in the global economy. It is his view that while countries like Japan and Germany are focusing on the creation of electronic data bases we are still preoccupied with buckram bindings and acid-free paper. According to Messner, people today don't want to read hard copy books any more than they want to wear knickers and bloomers. "It's a matter of image and style," is how Kulavian expressed it in his recent publication, *Hyperfashions,* a book whose hard copy sales have reached 3.5 million.[2]

Interestingly enough, however, you can find some of the staunchest supporters of the book among our profession's growing ranks of video librarians. It is becoming increasingly obvious to these audiovisual professionals that the alarming increase in functional illiteracy is a main reason why 73 percent of all Americans experience difficulty and frustration in operating a standard VCR.

So you don't think that the book is facing imminent extinction and that librarians will primarily become electronic information surfers?

No, of course not. People have been predicting the death of the book since the beginning of the twentieth century and the irony is that each year the number of books published worldwide increases.

To prove this point, let's get on our time machine, shall we, and travel to the city of St. Louis on a warm September afternoon in 1904. What's all the hustle and bustle, you ask? We've landed in the middle of the World's Fair, but please keep your voices down. We're here to listen to that stuffy little man with the funny accent talk about libraries. His name is Guido Biagi, and he's the internationally renowned librarian of the Royal Library of Florence, Italy. The paper he is delivering to the International Congress of Arts and Sciences is entitled "The Library, Its Past and Future."

It sounds like we missed the first half of his speech, the part about the past because just listen to this little guy talk: "There will be few readers, but an infinite number of hearers, who will listen from their homes to the spoken paper, to the spoken book. University students will listen to their lectures while they lie in bed, and will not know their professors even by sight. Writing will be a lost art. Professors of paleography and keepers of manuscripts will perhaps have to learn to accustom their eye to the ancient alphabets. Autographs will be as rare as palimpsests are now. Books will no longer be read, they will be listened to; and then only will be fulfilled the famous saying, the librarian who reads is lost."[3]

So there you have it—in the wake of the invention of the phonograph machine, the world's leading library expert announces the death of the book.

Was Biagi the Marshall McLuhan of his time?

No, actually Guido Biagi was not the first person to ring the book's death knell. A guy named Octave Uzanne beat him to it a decade earlier in an article entitled "The End of Books." According to him the art of printing had reached its pinnacle with Nicholas Jenson and had been in a state of decline ever since. Actually Uzanne welcomed the book's death. To him reading was a phenomenon contrary to nature. It was an awkward exercise that quickly brought on weariness, and furthermore it distracted the eye from its main function—the contemplation of the beauties of nature. He, therefore, looked forward to the day when phonograph cylinders and discs would supplant the book as man's basic mode of communication.

Writing in 1894 he predicted that "Libraries will be transformed into phonographotecks, or rather, phonostereoteks; they will contain the works of human genius on properly labelled cylinders, methodically arranged in little cases, rows upon rows, on shelves. The favorite editions will be the autophonographs of artists most in vogue; for example, every one will be asking for Coquelin's Moliere, Irving's Shakespeare, and Salvini's Dante."[4]

Okay, so Guido Biagi and Octave Uzanne's crystal balls were a little bit foggy and the phonograph cylinder didn't replace the book, but don't our modern computer and video technologies pose a much graver threat to the long term health of the book?

Ah, the computer . . . the videotape . . . the book. They keep popping up in our minds in ever changing sequences like images on a Las Vegas slot machine.

The trick we keep telling ourselves is to pick one. What does the modern library really want to be? Which symbol do we want to define us? The computer symbolizes information, the videotape symbolizes entertainment, and the book symbolizes education.

Symbols, although not real, are important to us because they are so alluring. They attract us and distract us. They induce us to drink beverages that are not good for us, drive cars that we cannot afford, and wear clothes that don't fit us. Three of our largest industries—public relations, politics, and advertising—manufacture symbols. We even have an official national symbol—the dollar bill. America is the land where anyone can strike it rich.

But what is a library, especially in our rapidly changing high tech–post print world? Has the symbol that we have been associated with for over a century become obsolete? Has the book been supplanted by the computer terminal? In the 1980s growing numbers of librarians seemed to think so. Computers were to the 80s what cars were to the 60s—the ultimate symbol of identity, and it's interesting to note that much of the colloquial language of the automobile has been applied to computers—a powerful computer is said to have "a lot of horsepower" and you don't turn on a computer, you "take it for a spin."

It's no wonder, therefore, that in the 80s librarians were quick to celebrate the notion that Western civilization had evolved into an informational age in an electronically connected global village. After all, our libraries had always been an integral part of the national information network. People routinely looked to us for information on a diversity of subjects — analyzing the stock market, diagnosing an illness, baking a casserole, or tuning up a car. We functioned as a community information center even before the concept of an "information age" became fashionable.

But it's difficult to see, however, where things have changed now that we've entered the information age. We still get the same kinds of reference questions that we used to get back in the "industrial age." A casserole is still a casserole, and a V-8 engine is still a V-8 engine.

On a personal level, I keep reading about the knowledge explosion and about how my own personal informational needs are also exploding, but I'm still waiting for the explosion. Last week my washing machine broke down and I checked out a book on how to fix it. Last weekend my ten year old son needed three books to complete a school report on Ecuador. And last night my eighteen year old got a flat tire. I showed him step by step (never, ever tighten the lug nuts while the car is jacked up) how to change it just as my father had shown me twenty-five years earlier. We may live in a high tech world but we still stumble around in the same primitive way that Fred Flintstone and Barney Rubble did in the stone age. Public libraries exist today as they existed fifty years ago — to help people cope with a somewhat annoying and frustrating world. Does that make them information centers? No, that makes them libraries.

Having lived for ten years in the information age, librarians are beginning to realize this, and consequently we are beginning to understand the limitations of embracing the computer as a professional symbol. The novelty of the computer is starting to wear thin. As a personal tool, it has not delivered the miracles that we were promised. It turns out that the computer won't balance your checkbook, won't write your personal thank you notes, and won't do your income taxes for you. Certainly it can help you do these things, but why bother. It's easier to do them the old fashioned way — with pencil and paper.

In short, home computers have really not revolutionized our personal lives, with one major exception. They do make wonderful video game machines. I would be willing to guess that the average home computer is used more for game playing than any other function, which means one very important thing — America has not entered the information age after all. It is the age of entertainment that we live in. Ours is a time period in which life and liberty have been supplanted by the pursuit of happiness as the great American civil right.

And now we librarians want to join in the fun. We've decided our patrons are no longer interested in knowledge, wisdom, learning, and inquiry. They're searching for fun instead. Our new symbol, therefore, is not the book or even the computer. It is the video cassette recorder.

But we may have picked the wrong symbol. The signs are all around us that America has had its fun, the party is over, and the tab has suddenly arrived. Falling test scores and proliferating illiteracy are the key items on the bill. The age of entertainment has created a new age, the age of ignorance. The richest nation in the world has become one of the least well educated.

This can only mean one thing. We are heading for yet another age — the age of education. I have a radical prediction — the book will be rediscovered as a revolutionary teaching tool. It's a symbol we just might want to be associated with.

Your prediction flies in the face of what all the country's leading futurists are saying. Why do you have so much confidence in the book?

The book is like the cockroach. It has been around for a long, long time and year after year and century after century it survives the challenge of the new technologies that threaten its very existence. It is versatile and adaptable to all cultures and all earthly conditions, and that is something that you cannot say about any other form of media from the papyrus scrolls and cuneiform tablets of the third millennium B.C. to the phonograph cylinders and CD-ROMs of the twentieth century A.D.

When I got into librarianship twenty-some years ago, the exciting new media formats were 8mm film loops and 8-track tapes. Today if any of these film loops or tapes have survived the passing of time (which is highly doubtful) they would be utterly worthless because you simply wouldn't be able to find any equipment in which to play them. The 8mm film loops were made obsolete by Super 8mm film loops which were made obsolete by video discs which were made obsolete by ¾ inch videotapes which were made obsolete by ½ inch Beta videotapes which were made obsolete by ½ inch VHS videotapes which will soon be made obsolete by high definition, digital videotapes. And how about those 8-track tapes that made reel-to-reel tapes obsolete? They were replaced first by cassette tapes and then by compact discs, which will both soon be replaced by digital tapes. And let's not forget about computers. Each new generation of computer hardware renders the previous generation of computer software useless. Historians bemoan the fact that millions upon millions of Pentagon documents on the Vietnam War are disintegrating on magnetic tapes that cannot be accessed by modern computers, and to compound the problem is the fact that the few antique computers that can access these tapes are no longer serviceable, which means, oddly enough, that World War II is a much better documented historical event than the Vietnam War!

The problem with nonbook materials is that they become worthless when the equipment needed to support them becomes obsolete. That is why if the book had been invented last month, everyone would be hailing it as a work of pure genius. I can see the reviews now in *Library Technology:* "Finally we have a full color, full text document format that needs no batteries, is portable, easy to handle, and can be read when you are sitting down, standing up, lounging in bed or taking a bath. It can also serve a number of other functions such as an interior decoration accessory, a prop to hold up a broken bed, a place to hide money, a tool to press leaves, and a missile to project at someone who is antagonizing you. No doubt about it, this new format will make floppy-disk and CD-ROM formats obsolete. No other medium today can match the book for its handiness and attractiveness."

What are the characteristics of a good library book collection?

The first thing I look for is dust jackets. Dust jackets represent everything that is good and user friendly about the book format. A well designed book jacket is colorful and inviting. It is to a book what clothes are to a person. If a book has no jacket at all or one that is drab, lifeless, and dated, then, yes, I would agree with Mr. Kulavian Messner that only a geek would want to be seen with such a book. On the other hand, a book sporting a jacket that is both colorful and attractive is the perfect clothing accessory for today's fashion conscious man and woman.

In fact a big problem with electronic books and journals is that they are by definition jacketless. In my opinion, the electronic book will not become popular until this problem is overcome. Current technology is obviously not up to the task.

Remember, our role as librarians is not just to make books accessible; we must also make them desirable. It is our job to not only lead the proverbial horse to water but also to make him drink. Just for fun try putting out two copies of The Joy of Sex on your new books display rack. Let one of them be a floppy disk copy and let the other be the famous book edition with its seductive jacket. Which format do you think will be checked out first? Fortunately, you don't have to speculate because hard data on this issue is already available. H. Alfred Steegmuller, a very inventive doctoral candidate at the Upper Michigan School of Information Studies, performed this experiment 750 times at various Detroit suburban libraries. His results were reported in a dissertation entitled, "Reading Format Choices: Experimental Discoveries about the Preferences of End Users in a Public Library Context."[5] In all but one case the jacketed book was the patron's format of choice, and it should be noted that the one person who selected the electronic disk was given a breathalyzer test which revealed an advanced state of ebriosity.

The book jacket issue is one of the main things that distinguishes public librarians from academic librarians. The average public librarian takes great pains to highlight and preserve book jackets, while the average academic librarian simply throws them away as though they were nothing more than the skin from a sausage. I find this to be wasteful, of course, but also quite censorious.

How extensive is book jacket censorship in the United States?

Although book jacket censorship is not something that you will read very much about in The Intellectual Freedom Newsletter, it is a very real professional problem, one that is beginning to get the attention of the ever observant editorial staff of the The Vigilant Librarian.

According to Dr. H. Somerset Roth in his article "The Dust Jacket Issue: Policy Decision or Institutional Censorship" there are basically two types of dust jacket censorship: (1) librarian-driven and (2) publisher-driven. Obviously librarian-driven censorship is most prevalent in academic libraries but the scary thing is that in the past few years it has begun to rear its ugly head in public and school libraries as well.

The average dust jacket censor justifies his dirty-work with the old adage, "You should not judge a book by its cover," but according to Dr. Roth this is strictly a cover-up. "In my opinion," he writes, "it is not literary prejudgment that the average dust jacket censor is concerned about, it is dust jacket nudity." By banning all dust jackets, the censor can hide behind the mask of policy and avoid having to engage in the embarrassing practice of banning morally objectionable jackets on a case by case basis.[6]

Professor Sylvia Samford-Gullickson, in her seminal work *Institutional Practices That Threaten Intellectual Freedom*, expresses serious concern about another, more subtle form of dust jacket censorship. She writes, "The data I gathered by examining the dust jackets of 87 specific titles in 53 different upstate New York libraries points clearly to a systematic and profession-wide practice of intentional book jacket defacement."[7] According to Samford-Gullickson this form of censorship occurs "whenever clerical personnel working in technical services attempt to cover up areas of dust jacket nudity with a library's property stamp."[8] She claims (with documented evidence) that she found 317 instances where bare breasts and/or buttocks had been property stamped by library personnel.

What's even more alarming is that a growing number of publishers have seemingly been pressured into not using jackets to cover their new releases. For example when the book *Mud through the Ages* was released last year did you notice that it did not have a jacket? Why? What did they have to hide? You tell me.

My position on the issue is clear. The book without a book jacket is covering something up. It's nothing more than the old game of hiding something inside a plain brown wrapper. Law books are a good example. They never have dust jackets. Why? The answer according to Herman Copenhaver, J.D., is elementary. In his treatise, *Barriers: How the Legal Industry Protects Itself*, he makes the startling claim that there is a conspiracy between lawyers and legal publishers to discourage the common person from reading law books. Copenhaver writes: "Law books are produced jacketless with drab, unappealing covers in order to make them as offputting as possible to the general reader. Obviously if people started writing their own wills, contracts, and pleas, this would cut significantly into lawyer profits."[9]

Copenhaver's point is equally applicable to the books serving other professions. Medical books, accounting books, real estate books, and even library science books (yes, that includes this one) are invariably produced without dust jackets. The last thing the medical profession wants is for Jacques the hair stylist or Joan the beautician to pick up a book on brain surgery and start doing barber-shop frontal lobe operations. Think of how much money is at stake. The same goes for librarianship. Show me a more physically unattractive book than AACR2. The point is we don't want laypeople poking around our professional trade secrets. It might make us expendable.

Is there a movement afoot in the library profession to pressure publishers to provide more dust jackets?

Dust jacket advocates have, of course, been around for many years. Unfortunately their cause has taken a back seat to those librarians who are more concerned about pressuring publishers to give libraries a larger percentage discount on book purchases.

However, from time to time, attempts have been made to interest the ALA's Executive Board in the dust jacket issue and in 1984 a committee was formed to study the problem. After five years of meetings and hearings, the BCAC (Book Coverings and Accoutrements Committee) issued a 700-page report (which incidentally was not jacketed and was therefore not widely read).

Among other things, the report stated that dust jackets are an integral part of the book format as we know it today. The report states that "Dust jackets are as important to a book as an index or a table of contents. Librarians should no more throw away a dust jacket than they should tear out and throw away the final twenty pages of the book itself."[10]

The most valuable part of the report expressed the strong sense of the committee that "book reviewers who write for library trade journals should boycott publishers who do not provide dust jackets with all of their books."[11]

But isn't the dust jacket the last thing a reviewer should consider in evaluating a book?

Au contraire. The jacket itself sets the tone for the book. When you get dressed you are doing more than just keeping yourself warm, dry, and decent. You are consciously or unconsciously creating an image. You'll wear one thing to a job interview, another thing to the beach, and still another thing to go bungee jumping. When someone sees you in a three piece suit they're not going to say, "Hi, I hope you have fun bungee jumping today!" They're going to ask, "Where's your job interview?" or "Whose funeral are you going to?"

The same holds true with the dust jacket. It is no coincidence that we use the term "jacket." As the book's clothing it does more than provide protection. It sends us a signal about the book's purpose and personality. In her article, "Deconstructing Dust Jackets," Dr. Hillary M. Dubois explores the psychological impact that dust jackets have upon their readers. According to Dubois, a properly designed dust jacket uses colors and shapes to put the reader into just the right mood to enjoy and appreciate the book contained within. "It's a little like foreplay," writes Dr. Dubois, "in that the book's author is, in a sense, trying to engage the reader's most intimate attention." Dubois goes on to state that her research reveals that "there is a direct relationship between the creativity of a dust jacket and the sense of focus that the reader brings to the book."[12]

Oddly enough what Dr. Dubois also discovered is that while a dust jacket's color and artistic style are certainly important in stimulating a psychological response, most readers focus first on the photograph of the author. Extending the analogy of the sex act, Dubois claims that different readers are attracted to different author pictures, and that if a reader has a negative feeling about an author based upon the dust jacket photo, nothing (not even a great review) will motivate that reader to surrender a sense of intimacy to the book.

Does this research finding have any implications for book selection?

Absolutely. It means that we must diversify. Certainly balance and variety have always been the benchmarks of a good library collection. But traditionally we have defined balance and variety in terms of style, content, and subject area. Dr. Dubois' research forces us to rethink these parameters. We must also include dust jacket author photos in our list of selection criteria.

Practically speaking, this means that we should collect books by authors of varying physical appearance. For instance, we need to insure that our collections contain books by fat authors and skinny ones; mean-looking authors and pleasant-looking ones; beautiful authors and ugly ones (with every variation in between). Obviously it becomes important for book reviewers to describe the author as he or she appears on the dust jacket photo.

Are certain types of authors more fit for certain subject areas?

Yes. In an article that appeared recently in *The Anglo-American Library Review* Frederick Anselm reports on some interesting work he did building upon the research of Dr. Dubois. What Anselm did was take a series of eight photographs of various everyday, noncelebrity people and show them to 150 randomly selected library patrons in Orange County, California. Each of the patrons was asked a series of 75 questions about each photograph — Would you read a cookbook by this person? Would you read a mystery by this person? Would you read an auto repair manual by this person?

Obviously Anselm ended up with mountains of data. When it was all collated and correlated he was able to make a number of statistically significant conclusions too numerous to repeat here. However the important point remains — library patrons do to a large degree base their selection decisions upon the dust jacket author photo. For example, patrons seem to prefer to read cookbooks by fat people, mysteries by skinny people, sex manuals oddly enough by men and women tending toward ugliness, and scholarly books by people with a scholarly, elitist look about them — you know, pipes and bow ties and wire framed spectacles, that sort of thing.[13]

But is there a place for elitism in book collection development?

There's as much of a place for elitism as there is for populism. Book collection development is, as E.K. Chang puts it, "strictly a yin and yang proposition."[14] Hey we're all human beings. We need wisdom; we need entertainment. I'd never want to sit next to somebody at a dinner party who hadn't read at least a little of both Dante and Danielle Steele. Don't discount the fact that it's not easy trafficking in the human condition so close to the beginning of a new millennium.

We need to know something about particle physics as well as micro-wave cooking to get along in a passable manner.

The best libraries, therefore, are the most diversified libraries. The libraries that put too much focus on any one area, like high demand bestsellers, are actually practicing a most pernicious form of censorship. They limit people's horizons instead of expanding them.

But isn't it overly elitist to invest money in books that only a small part of the library's population has the interest or ability to read?

Again I quote Dr. Chang: "The worth of a book is in its use." In his recent article, "Value Neutrality and the Death of the American Library,"[15] Chang asks us to reflect upon the person who reads a new translation of Kierkegaard's obscure nineteenth-century work *Concluding Unscientific Postscript,* and experiences something very close to spiritual enlightenment. From this uplifting experience flows a lifetime of good works and charity to mankind. Chang then poses the question, "Given this result, isn't the seldom checked out book by Kierkegaard more valuable than a fifteenth copy of a Stephen King thriller that will produce only three or four hours of fleeting entertainment for its many readers?"[16]

If posing moral dilemmas such as this is elitism, then by all means call me an elitist. The fact of the matter is, the librarians who buy only popular materials are the true elitists because they cynically think that the common man cannot understand or enjoy anything more sophisticated than lawyer novels or yuppie love stories. On the other hand, elitist librarians also have their more supercilious side. They are, after all, maddeningly elitist.

What are the advantages and disadvantages of having cultural elitists on a library staff?

In his book *Good Things About Bad People and Bad Things About Good People,* Rabbi M.C. Hammerstein identifies the following good and bad things about elitist librarians:

FIVE BAD THINGS ABOUT ELITIST LIBRARIANS

1. They tend to talk very metaphorically at baseball games about how the pitcher's mound is a latent symbol of repressed sexuality and the stadium itself is a microcosm of Creation.
2. While you're reading *People* magazine during your coffee break, they come into the staff lounge and say, "Lately I've been slumming with Thackeray. After all it is summer."
3. They talk as if a dirty database is somehow a staff health threat.
4. At happy hour they tend to say things like, "Did you know that one bottle of beer can kill two million brain cells," and they say it in such a way as to imply that you definitely don't have two million brain cells to spare.
5. They often invite you to go to the opera with them.

FIVE GOOD THINGS ABOUT ELITIST LIBRARIANS

1. They are always willing to share the jar of Grey Poupon that they leave on the staff room lunch table.
2. Sometimes they don't finish eating their little carton of Häagen-Dazs and they let you scrape the bottom of the container.
3. They relate very well to the many college professors who double as problem patrons.
4. They never hesitate to lecture parents of unruly children.
5. They are handy to have around when some pseudointellectual in horn rims and a pipe walks up to the reference desk and says, "I'm looking for something in the area of minimalist literature that will, you know, speak to me in a very real way."[17]

So what's the last word on books?

Books are among the handiest and most enduring artifacts invented by human beings. Instead of using technology to try to supplant them, why not use technology to enhance them? Why can't publishers be persuaded to find new ways to make them sturdier and even more attractive than they already are?

Notes

1. Ignatius Mendleson Godbehare, *Zen Libraries and the Birds of Appetite* (Boston: Wittleson and Franklin, 1991), p. 27. Godbehare's other book on library architecture, *Nada, Dada, and Dewey*, is also an interesting introduction into the concept of bibliotechnical nihilism. In it he talks about the "library of emptiness" where there are no books to distract the patron from "processing meditative data."

2. Kulavian Messner, *Hyperfashions* (New York: Torkleson Books, 1992), p. 13. While hard copy sales of this book have reached 3.5 million, disk sales are stuck at 17.

3. "Library Section, St. Louis International Congress of Arts and Sciences," *Library Journal* (October 1904) 530. The reaction of the editors of *LJ* to the speech given by Professor Biagi is worth noting. It appears on page 515 of the issue cited above. They translated the essence of his talk into the following question: "Are we to have no more books, in the printed sense, and are we to return to a modern version of Babylonian bricks, in the shape of phonograph records?" Unlike Biagi, the editors were disposed to answer the question in the negative. Although admitting that phonograph records and the phonograph itself would become a standard feature of libraries, they adamantly refused to accept the proposition that an author's reading, recorded by the phonograph, would be the most satisfactory method of presenting the written word. Ultimately the editors felt that there were three observations of a strictly practical nature that would save the printed book from obsolescence. They were (1) storage, for it was felt that phonograph records would take up far more room than print, (2) expense, and (3) the belief that the eye is a superior organ to the ear, and could in a few seconds sweep a page where minutes would be required for the hearing sense. The *LJ* editors, therefore, wisely concluded that "we cannot follow Professor Biagi in his aerial flight, nor advise that the shelving of the modern stack shall be turned into warehouse bins for phonograph records."

4. Octave Uzanne, "The End of Books," *Scribner's Magazine* (August 1894) 225.

5. Harvey Alfred Steegmuller, "Reading Format Choices: Experimental Discoveries about the Preferences of End Users in a Public Library Context," a dissertation in partial fulfillment of the D.L.S. at the Upper Michigan School of Information Studies (1989).

6. Hubert Somerset Roth, "The Dust Jacket Issue: Policy Decision or Institutional Censorship," *The Vigilant Librarian* (spring 1989) 57–62.

7. Sylvia Samford-Gullickson, *Institutional Practices That Threaten Intellectual Freedom* (Oklahoma City: Panhandle Press, 1987), p. 57.

8. *Ibid.*, p. 63.

9. Herman Copenhaver, *How the Legal Industry Protects Itself* (Berkeley: Swearington and Associates Press, 1988), p. 153.

10. Book Coverings and Accoutrements Committee of the American Library Association, *The Book Dust Jacket: Its History, Its Present, and Its Future* (Library Publications, Inc., 1984), p. 666.

11. *Ibid.*, p. 699.

12. Hillary M. Dubois, "Deconstructing Book Jackets," *The Contemporary Librarian* (December 1989) 34.

13. Frederick Anselm, "Patron Perceptions of Dust Jacket Author Photos," *The Anglo-American Library Review* (spring 1990) 93.

14. Chang, E.K., "Zen and the Art of Library Book Selection," *New Age Librarian* (July 1985) 227.

15. Chang, E.K., "Value Neutrality and the Death of the American Library," *Journal of Library Ethics* (autumn 1988) 17.

16. *Ibid.*, 19.

17. Moses Cohen Hammerstein, *Good Things About Bad People and Bad Things About Good People* (Garden City, NJ: Mount Sinai Press, 1990), p. 45.

REFERENCE

Lady, let me get this straight. You want me to tell you how to say "Good morning" in sign language over the phone?

What exactly is the reference interview?

According to C. Johanson Doppelgäng in his book *Mastering the Art of Reference Conversation*, the reference interview is the communication process by which a librarian determines what exactly a patron wants.[1] It sounds like a simple process, but most researchers will tell you that it is actually a very complex and convoluted communication challenge that requires a great deal of professional training.

For example, let's say a man comes into your library and asks, "Does this library have any books on dogs?" The conventional wisdom is that this man simply wants you to give him the proper classification number for dogs and some simple instructions of how to get there. However, according to Professor Frances Starke of the Minnesota State University Graduate School of Librarianship that is often not the case. Her contention is that the reference patron is often a deeply disturbed individual crying out for attention and understanding. "It is sad but true," she writes, "but in many cases it would be far more appropriate to have a psychiatrist's couch at the reference desk rather than a simple chair."[2] She spent five years studying this issue in five large Midwestern libraries, and in the course of this research she observed over 5,000 different reference interviews.

In her provocative and controversial book, *Why Library Patrons Lie*, Starke claims that 87 percent of the people who seek assistance at the reference desk are not completely honest about what they want, and she says that this duplicity stems from a wide diversity of reasons — patrons may be pursuing illegal activities, they may not want to divulge personal information about themselves, they may be afraid of a value judgment from the reference librarian, and they may be very concerned about not wanting to appear to be stupid.

In the course of her five years of research, Starke observed the exact question, "Does this library have any books on dogs?" five times. After each reference transaction was completed, she met privately with the patron and conducted her own in-depth interview. She found the following:

1. One patron wanted information on the nutritional value of hot dogs.

2. One patron was attracted to the reference librarian and simply wanted to engage her in a conversation in hopes of obtaining a phone number and a date.

3. One patron was looking for an unobtrusive method to kill his neighbor's dog.

4. One patron was looking for a way to breed his cocker spaniel with his Siamese cat.

5. One patron was looking for the best way to cook dog meat.[3]

What is the proper way to conduct a reference interview?

This question is best answered by indicating the improper way! Dr. Susan Abrams Stubbs, in a recent journal article entitled "Negotiating the Reference Interview—A How Not to Guide," indicates that a common mistake that many reference librarians make is to get too involved, too judgmental, and too personal with the patron. She writes, "Maintaining professional detachment is absolutely critical at all times."[4] In the following examples Dr. Stubbs describes five hypothetical reference scenarios and gives us the wrong way and the right way to deal with each of these very touchy situations.

1. A patron comes into the library and says, "Last night in the check-out line of the supermarket I read a newspaper article that said that a man in the Philippines gave birth to a five pound chimpanzee last month. Can you find some more information about this event?"

Do Not Say: "That is the stupidest question I have gotten in my twenty-five years of working the reference desk! How dense can you possibly be. Don't you know that the people who publish tabloids are the world's biggest con artists and that the only way they stay in business is because of idiots like you."

Do Say: "That's an interesting story. I'll show you where the magazine indexes are so that you can research it further."

2. A patron comes up to the reference desk and says, "I have a lump in my abdominal area. Can you help me determine what exactly it is?"

Do Not Say: "Please step back into the reference office, take off your clothes, and I'll be back there in a few minutes with a medical dictionary to give you a thorough physical exam."

Do Say: "As a librarian I am not qualified to make a medical diagnosis, however, I can show you where our medical reference collection is."

3. A patron asks, "I'd like to know where I can obtain information on how to make an explosive device strong enough to blow up a 2,600 square foot single family residence."

Do Not Say: "Look in the 355 series and when you find the information share it with me because my next door neighbor is driving me crazy too."

Do Say: "This is a highly irregular request but if you check the catalog you will find that the relevant subject heading is "Explosives." You might also want to check under "Explosives—Laws and Legislation" and "Explosives—Safety Measures."

4. A patron says, "I am doing a research paper on sexual inadequacy in men. Do you have any information on this topic?"

Do Not Say: "Oh just admit the truth—you're impotent aren't you? That's the first step—to face up to the problem and to understand that it is no shame to be impotent. Modern science has done wonders with this problem. We have plenty of books that will help you. I also know a woman who might be of some assistance. What did you say your name was?"

Do Say: "We have a wealth of information on this subject. You can start your research by going to the classification number 616.69, which you will find located on the main floor of the nonfiction section."

5. A patron says, "My dentist has scheduled me for a root canal operation. I would like information on this procedure."

Do Not Say: "What do you need to know? I had one done last summer and it was the most pain I've ever been in. It's even worse than having a baby. They stick these long sharp files right into the nerve of your tooth. It's like scraping the back of your eyeball with a piece of rough sand paper. But look at it this way—it's a good way to lose weight and you look like you could stand to lose at least twenty pounds."

Do Say: "We have several good books on modern dentistry that will give you a comprehensive description of the root canal procedure. I know this firsthand because they helped me understand the root canal that I had done last summer. Let me help you find them."[5]

What are the benefits of working in reference services?

Because reference is essentially a fact-finding function, most reference librarians are excellent at trivia games. According to the journal *Statistics Weekly,* 7 percent of the people who win television quiz shows have a background in reference librarianship.[6] This is quite impressive when you realize that reference librarians comprise only .067 percent of the total American workforce.

What are the hazards of working in reference services?

In his article "The Dysfunctional Reference Librarian," Siegfried Young, distinguished professor at the Melville Dewey School of Library Studies, identifies six common occupational hazards of working in the reference function:

> 1. The "Reference Librarians Who Research Too Much" Syndrome. This occurs when the reference search becomes obsessive, and the reference librarian simply loses control of his or her ability to bring a search to closure. Whenever you hear a reference librarian say, "I still haven't checked the 1947 edition of *Encyclopaedia Britannica*," it's a good bet that he or she is suffering from this problem. You will sometimes see this syndrome referred to in the literature as "infomania."
>
> 2. Information Overload. If ignorance produces bliss, then it stands to reason that information can produce depression. The more information that a reference librarian absorbs about the world, the more he or she can become chronically despondent. Over the course of a year the average reference librarian is exposed to literally thousands of informational details about diseases, famines, droughts, earthquakes, air pollution, water pollution, soil erosion, crime, war, and corruption. You can be sure that information overload is at work whenever you hear a reference librarian say, "Your new car is beautiful, but do you know that it will spew 40 tons of carbon monoxide into the earth's atmosphere just during the first week that you drive it and that if you keep the car for five years you will probably end up paying $9,500 in insurance premiums, $3,500 in gasoline, and $4,600 in maintenance and repairs, assuming you don't have an accident and total it, of which there is a 7 percent chance that you will."

3. Validation Deprivation. Because reference librarians do not make lucrative salaries, they look to their patrons for job satisfaction, and when patrons don't express some clear sign of appreciation, the librarian can experience a self-esteem disorder commonly referred to as "validation deprivation." Studies have shown that there is a direct relationship between the amount of time that a reference librarian spends on a research question and the amount of appreciation that the librarian needs to validate the experience. When you hear a reference librarian use any of the following terms to refer to a patron you can bet that a validation deprivation disorder is at work: geek, jerk, idiot, moron, numbskull, or cretin.

4. Intellect Retardation. Imagine buying a brand new Corvette with all the options and being able to drive it only in gridlock. That is how some reference librarians feel about their extensive academic training when they begin to realize that many of the questions that library patrons ask are of a rather ordinary and unchallenging nature. The effort put into high level courses on Boolean search strategies appears to be wasted when all your average patron seems to want is a simple stock quotation or the latest Stephen King thriller. The reference librarian suffering from intellect retardation can often be heard saying something like this to a patron: "You don't really want a book on cats, you want a book on the symbolic role of cats in the *Egyptian Book of the Dead* from the second millennium B.C."

5. Codependency. Because the reference librarian has a direct interface with the public there is a real danger of becoming codependent with some of the library's more addictive patrons such as the coupon clippers, the newspaper junkies, and the murder mystery addicts. When a reference librarian says to a patron, "I'll give you this new murder mystery by P.D. James now even though you're fifty-seventh on the reserve list because I know, appreciate, and can understand your need to be physically violent when you have to wait too long for a book," that's a clear signal that a codependent relationship has developed.

6. Nightmares. Extensive research shows that many people who work in reference suffer from the following four recurring nightmares:

(a) After spending four hours on a very difficult question and finally finding the answer, the reference librarian calls the patron only to be told, "Oh, thanks, but I don't need the information anymore."

(b) After spending four hours on a very difficult question and finally deciding that the information is simply not available, the reference librarian calls the patron and is told, "Oh, thanks for the effort, but a librarian at Glendale Public found the answer for me in fifteen minutes."

(c) The reference librarian is brought before a judge for some unnamed crime. The judge finds the librarian guilty and says, "For your punishment you will be assigned to the Cataloging Department for five years without parole."

(d) The reference librarian gets a phone call from a local tavern where two men are having a heated argument about who won the 1980 World Series. After checking the *Baseball Encyclopedia* the librarian goes back to the phone and informs the callers that the correct answer is the Philadelphia Phillies. Later that night as the librarian drives around the corner to her home she sees a large, bearded man on a motorcycle in her driveway wielding a tire iron.[7]

Dr. Young emphasizes in his book that if any one or two of these six occupational hazards becomes manifest in a reference librarian's behavior pattern there is no reason for immediate concern. However, he does indicate that they could be symptomatic of a larger "burn-out" problem.

What exactly is reference burnout?

Although much research has been done on the subject, it is difficult to find a consensus of professional opinion on this subject. Some psychologists and library scientists feel that the whole concept of reference burnout is an illusion created by therapists and counselors desperate for new syndromes to treat. According to Edwin A. Rourke, director of the Pickering Institute of Bibliosociotechnical Studies, "The whole notion of reference burnout was created by a number of unscrupulous therapists wanting to capitalize on the fears and insecurities of post-industrial librarians."[8]

While Rourke's views have some acceptance among classically based psychologists, the fact is that the growing research being done in this area indicates a very real problem. More than anyone else, Dr. Gloria D. Ignus has studied burnout among reference librarians. She is the author of the groundbreaking work *Reference Stress Syndrome:*

Identifying It, Understanding It, Reversing It, and Preventing It, and we have gotten her permission to reprint the passage from her book describing the behavioral symptoms of this type of burnout:

THE 26 TELLTALE SIGNS OF REFERENCE BURNOUT

If you are a reference librarian you know that you are suffering from burnout when:

1. A fat patron asks for the latest diet book and you hand him/her a refrigerator lock.

2. You begin integrating primal scream therapy into the reference interview process.

3. You find yourself volunteering to file pocket parts into law books just to avoid public contact.

4. You suggest in a library staff meeting that it might be a good idea to start a staff exchange program so that reference librarians can have an opportunity to work in the cataloging department.

5. You begin saying, "It is not the role of the reference librarian to answer personal questions" whenever a patron asks you where the bathroom is.

6. You begin conducting reference interviews in pig Latin.

7. You stop bathing and using deodorant so that patrons will respect your space needs.

8. You begin hanging around people with contagious diseases in hopes that you will have an opportunity to start using some of your accumulated sick leave.

9. You start putting rubber snakes on top of the reference desk in order to scare away patrons.

10. You preface every reference interview with the question, "Is this going to take long?"

11. You arrange a pile of unabridged dictionaries on top of the reference desk so that you cannot be seen.

12. You start laughing hysterically when someone asks you for the book *Do It Yourself Plumbing.*

13. You begin wearing a button that says, "REALITY IS AN ILLUSION CAUSED BY A CHOCOLATE DEFICIENCY."

14. You say in a very loud voice in front of a lot of people, "What specific sexual problem do you have?" in response to a patron who asks you where he can find the book *Human Sexual Inadequacy.*

15. You find yourself hunting pigeons with a shotgun in the city park next to the library during lunch break.

16. You preface all reference encounters by sneezing into the patron's face.

17. As soon as you see a patron approach you pick up the phone and pretend to carry on a long-winded reference interview until the patron gets restless and leaves.

18. You develop an immediate bladder problem the minute you sit down at the reference desk.

19. Your supervisor begins leashing you to the desk to limit your wandering room.

20. A patron asks you for a good mystery and you hand her a copy of the Dewey Decimal System.

21. You carry on fantasy phone reference interviews with Hollywood stars.

22. You find yourself giving serious thought to running for an A.L.A. office.

23. You secretly make funny faces behind the backs of patrons whom you despise.

24. You rearrange the reference collection by color.

25. At lunchtime you begin eating raw onions and garlic to induce halitosis in order to keep patrons away.

26. You urge your director to install a trap door in front of the reference desk as a handy way to get rid of problem patrons.[9]

How does reference burnout impact the behavior of its victims?

Dr. Ignus found that when five or more of the above symptoms occurred at any one time, the reference librarian in question could definitely be diagnosed as having "burned out." While Ignus does not deal with the various levels of reference burnout, Harold Dorkson, M.L.S., in his article "The Three Degrees of Reference Burnout," does. He claims that first degree burnout is characterized by sleeping and eating disorders, second degree burnout manifests itself in violence to inanimate objects (photocopiers, computer terminals, and staff lounge vending machines), and third degree burnout results in erratic interpersonal behavior (knocking people's hats off, cutting their ties, or squirting water into their faces).[10]

What can be done to help librarians suffering from reference burn-out?

While in Dorkson's opinion counseling is sufficient treatment for first and second degree burnout, he recommends a more unorthodox approach for a librarian who has been scorched at the third degree level. Surprisingly, Dorkson makes the claim that the traditional treatment of rest, relaxation, and time off from work is actually very counterproductive. "A vacation," he says, "actually exacerbates the victim's feeling of job alienation."[11]

After spending a week on the beach in Maui and five days on a cruise to the Cayman Islands, the stricken reference librarian often experiences increased difficulty in dealing with problem patrons, frustrating reference questions, and inadequate bibliographical resources. Quality leisure time serves to dramatize the librarian's sense of dissatisfaction with his everyday job. After fishing for marlin in the Gulf the average on-line search loses its sense of adventure.

The most effective form of therapy, therefore, would be for the reference librarian to engage in leisure time activities that are more unpleasant and more stressful than what he or she would ordinarily encounter in the library. In other words, according to Dorkson, the burned out librarian should do something away from the library that will make reference work seem idyllic by comparison. Listed below are some of Dorkson's ideas:

HOT VACATION IDEAS
FOR BURNED OUT REFERENCE LIBRARIANS

1. A cruise through the Panama Canal on a gunboat during periods of civil unrest.
2. A tour of the remains of the Chernobyl nuclear generating plant.
3. A skindiving expedition in the Cleveland River.
4. A picnic in the South Bronx at midnight.
5. A Fourth of July celebration in downtown Baghdad at noon.

HELPFUL PART-TIME JOB HINTS
FOR BURNED OUT REFERENCE LIBRARIANS

1. Cleaning cars used by contract killers.
2. Waiting on tables in a biker bar.

3. Collecting overdue bills for a loan shark.
4. Working as the night janitor at a hazardous waste dump.
5. Working as a circulation clerk at a nearby public library.

GOOD VOLUNTEER OPPORTUNITIES
FOR BURNED OUT REFERENCE LIBRARIANS

1. Circulating gun control petitions at a country and western bar.
2. Passing out literature on the dangers of secondary smoke at a truck stop.
3. Giving retirement seminars to prisoners with life sentences.
4. Promoting natural childbirth classes at a retirement home.
5. Providing mediation services to street gangs.[12]

Dorkson feels quite strongly that any of the fifteen recommendations listed above will send the burned out librarian running and screaming back to book reviews, problem patrons, and Boolean searching in no time at all.

What happens if the burned out reference librarian does not respond positively to treatment?

Although there is no clinical term for extended reference burnout, noted *Library Review* columnist Sarah Bottomley refers to victims of long-term burnout as "roasted." According to her the roasted reference librarian needs time, understanding, and love, and should above all else, be kept away from the departmental paper cutter. Her recommendation is to assign this person the task of compiling bibliographies on plumbing books.[13]

Notes

1. Carlson Johanson Doppelgäng, *Mastering the Art of Reference Conversation* (Knoxville: McDougall and Sons Publishers, 1985), p. 247.
2. Frances Starke, *Why Library Patrons Lie* (Orono, ME: Whitely Press, 1986), p. 51.

3. *Ibid.*, p. 69.

4. Susan Abrams Stubbs, "Negotiating the Reference Interview—A How Not to Guide," *Journal of American Reference Studies* (spring 1990) 83.

5. *Ibid.*, 85–87.

6. Thelma Reddington, "T.V. Quiz Show Statistics," *Statistics Weekly* (September 24, 1991) 15.

7. Siegfried Young, "The Dysfunctional Reference Librarian," *Journal of American Reference Studies* (winter 1991) 119–122.

8. Edwin Alfred Rourke, "The Reference Burnout Myth," *The Contemporary Librarian* (February 1992) 227.

9. Gloria D. Ignus, *Reference Stress Syndrome: Identifying It, Understanding It, Reversing It, and Preventing It* (Galesburg, IL: Mental Heath Press, 1991), pp. 57–60.

10. Harold Dorkson, "The Three Degrees of Reference Burnout," *Journal of American Reference Studies* (spring 1992) 69. It should be noted that Dr. Sharon H. Copperpot has provided an alternative view on the issue of the levels of reference burnout in an article entitled "Reference Burnout Is Not Simply a Bad Day at the Beach," in which she is critical of Dorkson's "three degrees" analysis. She feels that the long term effects of acute burnout are more serious than he has suggested and the labels that she gives the three stages ("burnout, bubble-over, and melt-down") reflect this view. This article can be found on pages 34–59 in the summer 1993 issue of the *Journal of American Reference Studies*.

11. *Ibid.*, 72.

12. *Ibid.*, 73–74.

13. Sarah Bottomley, "At the Reference Desk," *Library Review* (summer 1992) 13.

CIRCULATION

What makes the circulation function so critical to the American library?

"The American library," writes noted historian Ellsworth C. Winchester in his monumental book *The Jeffersonian Ideal and the History of American Education,* "is predicated upon the very American notion that mankind is fundamentally good."[1] In his book, Winchester emphasizes that the concept that a library would not allow free access to all people but would also allow all people to take materials out of the building is uniquely American and perfectly reflective of the American spirit.

Herein lies the challenge that confronts us everyday. In a society that is falling apart from greed, corruption, and crime, it becomes more and more difficult to continue to see humankind as fundamentally good, and yet as librarians we are faced with that charge. As cities burn and banks collapse we continue to function under Jefferson's eighteenth century belief in the perfectability of men and women, and as we approach the year 2000 through the haze of smoke, fire, and smog, American library services continue to be free, open, and accessible to all.

An integral part of that function, of course, is the circulation of library materials. There is nothing else that we do that speaks as eloquently to the confidence that we have in our patrons. By allowing them not just to read our materials, but to take them home we are saying IN YOU WE TRUST.

What is the role of the circulation clerk in the modern American library?

In his recent book, *Managing the Modern American Library: A Contemporary Librarian Looks at His Outdated Profession,* A. Headly Riddlesworth makes the startling claim that no employee is more important to the success of a library than the circulation clerk. Besides pointing out the obvious—that as the point of first contact for most patrons, the circulation clerk must be warm, friendly, and personable—Riddlesworth also claims that the circulation clerk should have "a high degree" of expertise in the areas of data entry, record keeping, and conflict management. "A patron's overall disposition toward the library is often formed by how accurately his or her circulation record is maintained and how fairly his or her circulation issues are resolved."[2]

Because circulation clerks are among the lowest paid library employees, it is very difficult to find and keep good ones. In fact, Riddlesworth makes the surprising statement that he values "the proficient circulation clerk more than the proficient reference librarian because good reference librarians are much easier to recruit than good clerical employees."[3]

If circulation clerks are so important, why do they suffer such a poor reputation within the library profession?

Elizabeth H. Gencko, in her article "The Clerical/Professional Interface," reports on the extensive research that she did on the subject of how professional librarians feel about clerical staff and how clerks feel about professionals. Her findings reveal a wide attitudinal chasm between the two groups. Professionals tend to look down upon clerks, and clerks tend to resent professionals.

Although some of this enmity can be attributed to one's place in the organizational pecking order, Gencko claims that there exists an unusual sense of animosity between reference librarians and circulation clerks. She attributes much of this animosity to turf issues. Reference librarians hate it when a library patron approaches a circulation clerk with a reference question, and they become absolutely livid when the circ clerk attempts to answer the question instead of referring it to the reference desk. The frustration becomes even more unbearable when the circulation clerk answers the question correctly. By the same token, circ clerks despise reference librarians who philosophically refuse to reshelve a book even if it is sitting on the floor in the middle of an aisle.

Gencko concludes her article by regretting the reality that there doesn't seem to be any middle ground on the professional/clerical chasm. She writes, "Unfortunately circ clerks tend to describe reference librarians as 'lazy and arrogant' and reference librarians tend to describe circ clerks as 'ill-tempered and unpleasant.'"[4]

Is that a fair characterization? Are most circulation clerks ill-tempered and unpleasant?

Unfortunately, yes. Over time a circulation clerk can acquire a tough and hardened sense of disdain for the human race. "Let's put it this way," writes Francine M. Middlefinger in her article "Ringing Phones and Raging Patrons," "if you were to go out to dinner with a group of circ clerks and discuss the future of humankind you would discover a deep, dark, and ugly reservoir of pessimism."[5]

Dr. Middlefinger attributes this negativism to the fact that in the course of their jobs circulation clerks are subjected to a great deal of abuse from distraught patrons who are not happy with the library's rules and regulations regarding check-out periods, overdue fines, card blockages, residency requirements, and lost book fees. The average circ clerk starts out as a normal and well adjusted person. In fact my experience is that most circ clerks gravitate to library work because they are looking for a job in which they can enjoy a great deal of human interaction and validation. They want to help people and usually describe themselves as "people persons." But then shortly after they start their jobs many circulation clerks begin what Dr. Middlefinger calls the "Descent into Gloom." According to Middlefinger the Descent into Gloom entails the following seven traceable stages:

STAGE #1. *Enthusiasm.* The beginning circulation clerk may not realize that she is participating in what Professor Winchester would call a "great Jeffersonian experiment," but she does think that most people are good and that the library can help them to become even better. "I love the job of bringing books and people together" is something that a stage #1 circ clerk would definitely say.

STAGE #2. *Guarded Optimism.* About three weeks into the job, our circ clerk's good intentions are still intact, but her view of library patrons has become a bit tempered by an angry phone call or a rude encounter over an overdue book. "Why do some people have to be so unpleasant?" is the type of question that a stage #2 circ clerk might pose to a coworker during an afternoon coffee break.

STAGE #3. *Neo-Realism.* At about the three month mark, the typical circ clerk is beginning to lose the sense that working in a library is somehow more uplifting than, say, working in a bank or a department store. Not only is the circulation desk a constant flurry of activity providing little time for the appreciation of books, but library patrons don't seem any more civil or civilized than the average customer at a fast food joint. "It's a job," is what the stage #3 circ clerk says to her next door neighbor.

STAGE #4. *Disillusionment*. Five months into the job, our circ clerk is now beginning to think that working in a library may actually be worse than working in a fast food restaurant because at least at the restaurant most customers do not try to shirk paying their bill. In the library, however, it seems as though some people will say anything to avoid paying a nickel fine. "You look awfully healthy for someone who just had chemotherapy," is what the stage #4 circ clerk might very well say to an overdue patron claiming to have just gotten out of the hospital after a cancer operation.

STAGE #5. *Anger*. The duration from stage #4 to stage #5 is short. Six to eight weeks is about the average time it takes for the average circ clerk to feel the anger one feels after being betrayed time and again by supervisors and administrators who refuse to support their employees. The circ clerk will charge a patron $27 for losing a book, the patron will refuse to pay and will lie and say that he returned it in the bookdrop, the circ clerk will block the patron's card, the patron will scream and curse at the circ clerk and will then appeal her decision to the director, the director (in the name of good public relations) will give in to the patron, and finally the director will criticize the circ clerk for being "inflexible." At happy hour after a few drinks the stage #5 circ clerk can often be heard referring to the director as "a no good spineless wimp."

STAGE #6. *Hostility*. By the ninth month on the job, our circulation clerk, having given up on working within the system, is now beginning to seek alternative ways to penalize those overdue patrons whom the director has cowardly let off the hook. Usually there is nothing vicious involved unless you consider a deceased mouse in your mail box to be vicious.

STAGE #7. *Gloom*. After realizing that anger and hostility do no good, our once bright-eyed and bushy-tailed circ clerk sinks into a gloomy state of long term depression. She now sees everyone as a pre-varicator, a procrastinator, and a cheater. To the stage #7 circ clerk, the world is not a happy place, and only death can end our earthly pain.[6]

How many circulation clerks reach the dreaded seventh stage?

This is a matter of some conjecture and some controversy. In her article "Lies, More Lies, and Damned Lies: The Truth about Library

Circulation Clerks," Marian D. Hobby strongly disputes the assertions of Dr. Middlefinger that 30 to 40 percent of the people currently working in library circulation departments can be deemed to be clinically dysfunctional. As part of her effort to dispell the stereotype of the circulation clerk as a modern day harpy, Professor Hobby lists all of the rumors that have arisen about circulation clerks in the last three years for which she can find absolutely no supporting evidence:

ELEVEN FALSE RUMORS ABOUT CIRCULATION CLERKS

1. To toughen up their men, the U.S. Marines are planning to incorporate circ clerk field experience into their boot camp curriculum.

2. Two out of every four circulation clerks is an avid fan of professional wrestling.

3. It is considered chic among circulation clerks to go new car shopping at surplus military vehicle auctions.

4. The favorite leisure time activity of circulation clerks is shooting pumpkins with beebee guns.

5. The California State Legislature has passed a new law prohibiting the sale of handguns to circulation clerks.

6. The National Association of Circulation Clerks is considering passing a resolution recommending to the International Olympic Committee that roller derby be accepted as an Olympic sport.

7. The United States Secretary of Defense has a bumper sticker on his limousine that says, "HELP BUILD A SAFER WORLD: KEEP NUCLEAR ARMS AWAY FROM CIRCULATION CLERKS."

8. Genghis Khan was a circ clerk for two years.

9. Jimmy Hoffa is alive and well and working as a circ clerk at the Brooklyn Public Library.

10. The movie *Terminator 4* will be shot on location in the circulation department of the Cleveland Public Library.

11. Three out of every five circ clerks subscribe to *Soldier of Fortune* magazine.[7]

Is there any way to tell if one of your circulation clerks is ready to commit a violent crime against an overdue patron?

Dr. Susan Stanforth Turley, who spent three years observing job stress in nonprofessional library workers in preparation for a doctoral thesis entitled "Occupational Stress Related Behavioral Disorders in Nonprofessional Library Employees: A Field Study in Seven Public Libraries in Suburban Cleveland," recommends that library managers should be trained to detect the following behaviors in circ clerks that might indicate the imminence of a psychotic episode.

THE FOLLOWING FIVE SIGNS INDICATE THAT YOUR CIRC CLERK MIGHT BE READY TO EXPERIENCE AN UN-FORTUNATE PSYCHOTIC EPISODE CULMINATING IN ONE OR MORE ACTS OF VIOLENCE:

1. The circ clerk spends hours deploring patrons who go to the director to weasel out of fines.
2. Polaroid pictures of some of these overdue patrons (with concentric circles drawn over their faces) begin showing up on the circ clerk's desk.
3. An "I DON'T BREAK FOR OVERDUE BORROWERS" bumper sticker suddenly shows up on the circ clerk's car, and out at the desk, the circ clerk begins wearing a yellow smile button with the words "MURDER HAPPENS" added to it in homemade red lettering.
4. The circ clerk tells one of the reference librarians that in order to complete a term paper on crime she needs a book on how to commit a murder without leaving a trace of evidence.
5. The circ clerk asks another reference librarian for reference materials on cremation for a term paper that she is writing on "Comparative Funeral Rites" for a sociology class.[8]

What is the best way to evaluate a circulation clerk's performance?

R. Philip Jonesberry wrote about a very creative evaluation technique in *Library World* several years ago. Jonesberry, a public library director in the Mississippi delta region, pays a professional actor, who is wearing a half-body cast, to (a) crawl up to the circulation desk, (b) apologize for returning a book three weeks late, and (c) beg for a fine waiver because of a broken spine. According to Jonesberry if the circulation clerk responds in any of the following ways he or she should definitely be given some remedial training:

1. "Do you mean to tell me that you let a little thing like a broken spine keep you from returning your library books on time?"

2. "Broken spine or no broken spine, you still owe $2.10."

3. "Do you have a note from your doctor?"

4. "Do I look like Mother Theresa?"

5. "If I waived the fine for you I've have to do it for everyone else with a broken spine."

6. "If I waived your fine it wouldn't be fair to all the other people with broken spines who pay their library fines."

7. "Waiving your fine would set a dangerous precedent."

8. "What do you think would happen to the library if every person with a broken spine stopped paying their library fines?"

9. "There's nothing in our official Board adopted circulation policy that excuses people with broken spines from paying their library fines."

10. "If I let you off the hook on this fine, I could get fired."

11. "Three people with broken spines paid their fines yesterday."

12. "It's not my fault you broke your spine!"

13. "The next thing you know someone will want their fines waived because they have the sniffles."

14. "How do I know that cast isn't fake?"

15. "If I waive your fine the next thing you'll be asking me to do is scratch the skin under your cast with a coat hanger."

16. "You probably broke your spine on purpose just to get out of paying your library fines."

17. "Is the I.R.S. waiving your taxes?"

18. "Do you know that while you were lounging in the hospital with your broken spine two people were waiting for these books?"

19. "You want me to waive the fine? Tell that to the little homeless boy that I collected two dollars from yesterday."

20. "I wouldn't waive these fines even if you were dead."[9]

In addition to performance evaluations should circulation clerks be given periodical psychological tests?

I like the simple written test that Harold D. Wilson, director of the Palmsgrove Community College Library, has been using on a long term basis with impressive results (one shooting in seven years) in his circulation department. This short diagnostic quiz features the following five questions:

1. Do you look forward to the excitement that a nuclear war would bring to the nightly news?
2. Do you intentionally use hair spray with fluorocarbons in order to help deplete the ozone layer and speed up global warming?
3. Do you enjoy watching televised executions?
4. Do you go to car races specifically to see crashes?
5. Would you welcome the extinction of the whale, the snail darter, and the poodle?

According to Wilson, in his article "It's No Shame to Need Counseling," if one of your circ clerks answers "yes" to two or more of these questions you should definitely refer that individual to a trained therapist.[10]

What other ways are there to get to know your circ clerks better?

Dr. Amelia Stuart Mudd, in her journal article "Fantasies: Windows into the Minds of Library Circulation Clerks," derides Wilson's quiz as a superficial sham and argues that if you really want to probe the mental fitness of a circulation clerk you need to examine his or her fantasy life. According to Dr. Mudd, our fantasies tell more about us than anything else. "The fantasy," she writes, "is uniquely the creation of its fantasizer."[11] In preparing her article, Mudd delved into the fantasies of over 150 different circulation clerks, and from these in-depth interviews she discovered that circ clerks spend an inordinate amount of their time fantasizing about the concepts of crime and punishment as applied to circulation situations.

"This phenomenon," writes Dr. Mudd, "is perfectly healthy. It is very constructive for people to mentally envision their work issues being resolved in a fair and just manner. This engenders feelings of hope and stimulates positive thinking." However Mudd also warns that fantasies involving "the violent resolution of work problems seem to signal a deeply troubled and possibly dangerous mindset."[12]

For example, Dr. Mudd says that a common fantasy of circulation clerks is a scenario in which an army of circ clerks surround the home of an overdue borrower. One of the circ clerks is holding a bullhorn and is saying in a loud voice, "WE'VE GOT YOUR HOUSE SURROUNDED. IF YOU THROW YOUR LIBRARY BOOKS OUT THE WINDOW WE

WON'T SHOOT!" The deadbeat then obediently surrenders the books and no violence occurs. For Dr. Mudd this kind of a fantasy is good because it eschews a violent climax. However, if the fantasy were to result in gunfire between the circle of circ clerks and the deadbeat borrower there would be reason for concern.

Perhaps the most interesting finding that Dr. Mudd drew from her research was that there seems to be an unusually apocalyptic aspect to many circ clerk fantasies. In these fantasies, deadbeat borrowers are held accountable by some higher being for their library misdeeds. In some of these dreams the higher being is Yahweh and in others it is Jesus. This obviously reflects the Judeo-Christian background of most circulation clerks.

Usually these "accountability fantasies" take place in the context of a very frightening yet traditional "Last Judgment" scene held in the aftermath of a cataclysmic event of global proportions — often a world-wide earthquake measuring 17 or 18 on the Richter scale or a thermonuclear war that envelops the earth. It is interesting to note that 43 percent of the circ clerks who had regular apocalypse fantasies indicated to Dr. Mudd that the world's end would be prompted by a sudden act from a Supreme Being and that 44 percent felt that it would be caused by man's inhumanity to man. The other 23 percent were not sure and had fantasies featuring both types of scenarios. What is even more interesting is that 82 percent of these circ clerks expressed a definite preference to die in a global cataclysm rather than in a quiet hospital bed with "tubes hooked up to their noses."

Furthermore Dr. Mudd discovered that reading apocalypse literature appears to be a popular leisure time activity among circulation clerks. Sixty-seven percent of the clerks who were interviewed were familiar with the works of Nostradamus and Edgar Cayce, and 48 percent said that their favorite part of the Bible is the Book of Revelation, which provides a vivid description of the Last Judgment.

Dr. Mudd found that the Last Judgment appears to be the focus of most apocalyptic circulation fantasies. Typically these fantasies follow the traditional format of the Book of Revelation — all the world's deceased stand before God who is reading through a large ledger book listing the deeds and misdeeds of all who have walked on earth. Invariably, however, in the circulation clerk's fantasy, the ledger book contains the library circulation records of all who have walked on earth, and God (in contrast to the weak spined library director) will tolerate no excuses about temporary insanity or automobile break-downs. Those who have unpaid fines or unreturned books are thrown into the lake of fire.

While Dr. Mudd indicates that within the library profession these types of fantasies tend to be unique to circulation clerks, she does not find them to be particularly alarming or unhealthy. In fact she thinks that in many cases they can be a positive job morale booster. Dr. Mudd writes, "In the long run it is helpful to the circulation clerk to believe that ultimately justice will be done and deadbeat borrowers will be punished."[13] In fact, Mudd provides documentation showing that circulation clerks who believe in the last judgment are far less likely to commit violence or illegal acts against library patrons.

What can be done to prevent circ clerks from wallowing in negative thinking about the world and its inhabitants?

More than anything, circulation clerks need to feel that they are understood and appreciated by their supervisors, administrators, and coworkers. Jonathan S. Philips, the director of the Gravel Point Public Library in Gravel Point, Texas, has for the past two years been spear-heading a movement to get established within the library profession a special recognition day for circ clerks. In an article that he penned for *Library Weekly*, Philips declares, "It is not the mighty secretary that we should be celebrating every year; it is the lowly circulation clerk who needs our recognition. Who in our industry gets less respect and less pay and yet who does more work?" Philips goes on to say that when possible circ clerks should be given special "bennies" such as covered parking spaces, personalized stationery, and chocolate kisses. "Never underestimate the power of chocolate to turn an unhappy person into a happy one," he writes.[14]

Notes

1. Ellsworth Carter Winchester, *The Jeffersonian Ideal and the History of American Education* (Wilmington, NC: Tidewater Press, 1979), p. 59.
2. Andrew Headly Riddlesworth, *Managing the Modern American Library: A*

Contemporary Librarian Looks at His Outdated Profession (Denton, TX: Library Management Publications, Inc.), p. 104.

3. *Ibid.*, p. 107.

4. Elizabeth H. Gencko, "The Clerical/Professional Interface," *Support Staff Quarterly* (fall 1987) 257.

5. Francine M. Middlefinger, "Ringing Phones and Raging Patrons," *Support Staff Quarterly* (winter 1989) 356.

6. *Ibid.*, 358–364.

7. Marian D. Hobby, "Lies, More Lies, and Damned Lies: The Truth about Library Circulation Clerks," *Support Staff Quarterly* (summer 1991) 179.

8. Susan Stanforth Turley, "Occupational Stress Related Behavioral Disorders in Nonprofessional Library Employees," a dissertation in partial fulfillment of the D.L.S. at the Lower Michigan School of Information Studies (1990), p. 57–58.

9. Randolph Philip Jonesberry, "Nontraditional Evaluation Techniques for Library Personnel," *Library World* (October 1988) 15–17. Jonesberry has been widely criticized since the publication of this article. Essentially he has been accused of using questionable entrapment techniques that exacerbate the stress of an already difficult job. A typical example of the rebuttal literature on this issue can be found in an article by Millard A. Ford entitled "Evaluation or Entrapment: A Re-examination of the Jonesberry Technique from an Ethical Perspective." This article appears on pages 79–88 of the winter 1990 issue of the *Journal of Library Ethics*.

10. Harold D. Wilson, "It's No Shame to Need Counseling," *Library Personnel Management Quarterly* (fall 1990) 136–137.

11. Amelia Stuart Mudd, "Fantasies: Windows into the Minds of Library Circulation Clerks," *Library Personnel Management Quarterly* (summer 1991) 91.

12. *Ibid.*, 93.

13. *Ibid.*, 107.

14. Jonathan Stansfeld Philips, "A Modest Proposal: Setting Aside a Special Day to Honor Circulation Workers," *Library Weekly* (May 16, 1992) 44.

CATALOGING

It's too bad Fred died. He was just beginning to understand *AACR2*.

Are catalogers necessary?

This is a tough one. Certainly no one can dispute the fact that the production of cataloging data is absolutely necessary to librarianship as we know it today, but this is not to say that catalogers are necessary. According to Dr. Louis P. Stuckey, the issue is much like chefs and food. In an article entitled "Cataloging in a Fast Food Society," he writes that with computerization and networking the need for local original cataloging has greatly diminished.

Just as we seem to prefer the convenience of popping preprepared food into a microwave oven, so we prefer to simply push a few buttons at a computer terminal and gain access to instant cataloging information. The individual artistry of cataloging is largely passé. According to Stuckey, local librarians today would no more think about cataloging their own books, than they would think about doing their own rebinding. Cataloging today is a mass manufacturing industry. There's no room for the little person. This is the age of K.F.C. — Kentucky Fried Cataloging.[1]

Where does that leave catalogers in contemporary librarianship?

It leaves them in a position of obvious vulnerability, especially when you consider how unloved catalogers seem to be in the first place. For many years, of course, public services librarians and catalogers have coexisted in an atmosphere of uneasy tension. Catalogers were blamed for being antisocial nitpickers who were singlehandedly responsible for giving librarians their less than flattering image, and now that cataloging has become a lost art the ridicule has intensified. A good example of this is the sometimes tasteless and other times tacky book by Miles Magadan Moorhead entitled *Dumb Cataloger Jokes*. What follows are some samplings from that book:

Q. What does it mean when a job ad asks for a "dynamic, live-wire librarian?"
A. Catalogers need not apply.

Q. How many catalogers does it take to screw in a light bulb?
A. None. Catalogers don't screw in light bulbs; they screw in Illumination Sources.

Q. How can you tell when you're in a cataloger's cemetery?
A. The tombstones are all arranged by Cutter number.

Q. What's the difference between a live cataloger and a dead one?
A. A pulse rate.

Q. When can you be sure that your kid is going to grow up to become a cataloger?
A. When he says, "Tell Johnny I can't come out to play today. I'm doing a retrospective conversion of my dinosaur books."

Q. When can you be certain that your blind date is a cataloger?
A. When she says, "Tell me about yourself. Are you a monograph, a serial, or a Festschrift?"

Q. When can you tell that a cataloger is underpaid?
A. When you see him standing by the side of the road with a sign that says WILL CATALOG FOR FOOD.

Q. When can you tell that the car in front of yours belongs to a cataloger?
A. When it has a vanity license plate that says "AACR2."

Q. When can you be certain that the guy sitting next to you at the bar is a cataloger?
A. When he turns to you and says, "In college I experimented with near beer, but now I'm strictly a club soda kind of guy."

Q. What's the best way to antagonize a cataloger?
A. Talk about Cheerios when the conversation turns to serials control.

Q. How can you tell that the corpse at a funeral is the body of a cataloger?
A. When you hear one of the mourners say, "Gee, Fred looks so lifelike."

Q. What do you call a cataloger who says "Hi" to you in the morning?
A. Talkative.

Q. What do you call a cataloger who says, "Hi, nice day" to you in the morning?
A. Verbose.

Q. What do you call a cataloger who says, "Hi, nice day, how are you?" in the morning?

A. A misplaced reference librarian.

Q. When do you know that the guy who's trying to pick you up in a bar is a cataloger?

A. When he says, "Hey, babe, come home with me and I'll show you some really creative main entries."

Q. How can you detect a couple of catalogers on their honeymoon?

A. They're the hitchhikers standing on the ramp to the interstate with a sign that says "L.C. OR BUST!"

Q. Why should a cataloger see a botanist?

A. To get treated for Dutch Elm disease.

Q. How do you know when your cataloger needs a vacation?

A. When he says, "Everything is beginning to look like a 333.33 to me."

Q. What is job stress for a cataloger?

A. Deciding between 817.96 or 817.967.

Q. When do you know that the meeting you've wandered into is a group therapy session for catalogers?

A. When you hear someone say, "I first started worrying about the distinction between a hyphen and a dash when I was fourteen."

Q. When do you know that the people seated at the table next to you in a restaurant are catalogers?

A. When they whip out their pocket calculators as soon as the waiter brings the check.[2]

Moorhead, feeding off of the instant success of *Dumb Cataloger Jokes,* then came out with another book that turned out to be as controversial as it was popular — *Theories on the Origin of Catalogers* — in which he speculated on the "puzzling mystery of where that rather strange little duck, the cataloger, came from."[3] In the book he develops four distinctly different possibilities and one unified theory, under the heading "Five Theories on the Origin of Catalogers":

1. LITTLE BANG THEORY. According to this hypothesis there was a little bang in the cosmos approximately five to six billion years ago caused by an explosion of gases. Immediately after the bang a high concentration of radiation occurred resulting in a fireball. From this

fireball little sparks broke off and were sent hurtling through outer space. Moorhead theorizes that these little sparks may have been catalogers who eventually landed on earth shortly before the founding of King Sennacherib's Library in Assyria in 704 B.C. The violent origin of catalogers posited under this theory accounts for their preference for a more quiet, stable, and sedentary existence here on earth.

2. THE INTERPLANETARY VISITATION THEORY. According to this theory, catalogers are actually aliens from another planet who have been sent to earth by some powerful being to "tidy things up a bit." This explains why catalogers are often difficult to communicate with and why they tend to stick together. They act differently and dress differently from the rest of us because they *are* different. It also explains why catalogers generally marry their own kind.

3. THE TEN LOST TRIBES OF ISRAEL THEORY. This theory says quite simply that catalogers belong to one of the ten tribes that were scattered to the four winds after Assyria destroyed Israel in 721 B.C. This theory is largely based upon the similarity in format of *AACR2* and the Book of Deuteronomy in the Old Testament.

4. THE LOST CONTINENT OF ATLANTIS THEORY. This hypothesis claims that catalogers are the survivors of Atlantis, the mysterious continent that was destroyed by a volcanic eruption that occurred in 1500 B.C. Underwater archeologists have discovered a peculiar nature to a number of sunken communities in the area off the coast of Greece where Atlantis is thought to have been located. In these communities can be found the remains of old stone signs saying, "STORE, GENERAL"; "CLINIC, MEDICAL"; and "LIBRARY, PUB-LIC."

5. GRAND UNIFIED THEORY. This theory basically links up the other four in a logical, sequential manner. Here's how it goes: Long, long ago in a star system remote from our own there was a little bang (caused by a powerful suprahuman being) that produced an explosion of little catalogers that grew in size as they were flung toward earth where they landed in Assyria in 750 B.C. with the mission of tidying up the written records of mankind. These catalogers were so successful in mating with each other and reproducing their own kind that they formed their own tribe which unfortunately was scattered to the four winds in 721 B.C. The tribe eventually settled in Atlantis and formed a whole civilization based upon cataloging. This civilization, however, disappeared mysteriously and the tribe was broken up. A few survivors,

however, courageously escaped this mysterious cataclysm and managed to integrate themselves in countries all over the known world.

With the advent of Kentucky Fried Cataloging how has the image of the cataloger changed?

Now the humor that is poked at catalogers centers much more around the whole obsolescence issue. This regrettable trend started with the book *101 Uses of a Used Card Catalog* and has continued with Leo Louis Hanks' recent book *101 Uses of a Dead Cataloger and 99 Uses of an Obsolete Cataloger.* In this book (which actually does have a serious purpose, to help administrators find gainful jobs for catalogers who have been replaced by machines), Hanks goes to great pains to differentiate between dead catalogers and obsolete catalogers. "Dead catalogers," he writes, "are dead. They have no feelings, and they are not ambulatory. Their uses, therefore, are limited to serving in capacities best suited to inanimate objects."[4] The following is a list of organizational roles appropriate for dead catalogers:

FIFTEEN PRODUCTIVE USES OF A DEAD CATALOGER

1. Bike Rack
2. Door Stopper
3. Speed Bump
4. Coat Rack
5. Sand Bag
6. Handicapped Ramp
7. Lawn Sculpture
8. Reading Room Coffee Table
9. Printer Stand
10. Bookend for Oversized Volumes
11. Projection Screen Holder
12. Prop for Halloween Story Hours
13. Car Companion to enable you to drive to library meetings in the car pool lane on the freeway
14. Scarecrow to keep flies away from the barbecue during library staff picnics
15. Library Night Watchman

While Hanks admits that some of these uses (lawn sculpture, bookend, scarecrow, car companion, and security guard) might also be appropriate for an obsolete cataloger, he thinks that there are other, more productive ways to deploy this type of employee. What follows are some of his suggestions:

FIFTEEN PRODUCTIVE USES
OF AN OBSOLETE CATALOGER

1. Making scratch cards out of obsolete catalog cards.
2. Acting as the monitor for the proper use of the staff lounge microwave oven.
3. Watering live plants.
4. Dusting fake plants.
5. Polishing the globe.
6. Keeping track of I.R.S. forms.
7. Filing pocket parts and loose leaf updates into reference books.
8. Sharpening pencils.
9. Putting newly sharpened pencils out at the computer terminals and index tables.
10. Cleaning out the pencil sharpener.
11. Getting doughnuts for staff meetings.
12. Driving discarded books to the city dump.
13. Cleaning out the coffee maker.
14. Flicking the lights on and off at closing time.
15. Putting trash cans under roof leaks.

Jokes aside, what is the future of cataloging in America?

The reality is that cataloging is a dying art. As much as catalogers like to deny it, local libraries simply cannot afford to provide cataloging data that are tailored to the needs of local communities, and this means that jobs for professional catalogers will almost surely become nonexistent. Those professionals lucky enough to continue to find jobs in technical services will basically function as managers charged with the responsibility of training and supervising clerical and paraprofessional staff to do routine and mundane tasks that are involved with the mechanical processes and systems of on-line cataloging.

There are many art forms whose disappearance has left America a poorer place. Is this the case with catalogers? Will their absence contribute to the deterioration of our quality of life?

No, a thousand times no! In an article entitled "The Death of the Original Cataloger," William Welford Wellington writes that the disappearance of the cataloger will result in a new and needed emphasis in librarianship. The new focus will be on the big questions (What is the role of the library in a post-industrial era?) and not the little questions (Should "Newark" be filed before or after "New York?").

Wellington argues that American librarianship has from its very beginnings been more concerned with bibliographic records than with books. This preoccupation with format rather than substance in Wellington's words has been "the single biggest contributor to the librarian's harpy image."[5] Finally, Wellington concludes his point with a fascinating question: "Isn't it interesting," he asks, "that the most famous librarian in American history—Melvil Dewey—was nothing more than a glorified cataloger?"[6]

How about the guerrilla warfare that some of the few remaining local catalogers are waging against the Library of Congress?

It's the equivalent of shotguns against cruise missiles. Tight budgets, eroding tax bases, and new technologies that greatly diminish the importance of subject headings doom the few remaining internecine cataloging wars. The trend toward Kentucky Fried Cataloging will never be reversed.

But won't we miss the idiosyncrasies of the local catalog?

Actually, local cataloging was never as original as its proponents thought it was. Yes, sometimes the subject headings were simpler and more popularly accessible than those created by the Library of Congress, but most local catalogers never got as down and dirty as they would have liked you to believe.

Zoe Shillington, before she retired from forty years of public library reference work, wrote an interesting and informative article entitled "Subject Headings I Would Have Welcomed." Shillington's point was that her library's catalog was of absolutely no help to her in answering some of the most common (and most frustrating) questions she had to deal with in her long career.

According to Shillington, "The reading tastes of middle America, whether we're willing to admit it or not, tend toward the bizarre, the grotesque, the scandalous, the pornographic, and even the savage. Although we like to think of the library as primarily an educational resource center, we do not like to think about some of the subjects in which our patrons wish to be educated. Our society's preoccupation with freak television — Oprah, Phil, Sally Jessie, and Geraldo — and trash television — "Hard Copy," "A Current Affair," and "Lifestyles of the Rich and Famous" — is a manifestation of this regrettable phenomenon."[7]

But while television producers and programmers have been more than willing to deal openly and honestly with America's tastes for the distasteful, catalogers never seemed to be able to bring themselves to the realization that there is something rather twisted in the American psyche. What follows is a list of some of the subject headings Shillington could have used at the reference desk:

1. Mass Murderers.
2. Serial Killers.
3. Mafia Hit Men.
4. Presidents with Scandalous Private Lives.
5. Famous Cannibals Who Served in Congress.

How about an obituary for the late, great cataloger?

We have come to both bury and praise catalogers. They tried valiantly to give dedicated service to their libraries and in many cases were heroically successful. The precomputer cataloger had the exacting task of reducing large volumes of information into a few spare subject headings. These professionals practiced minimalism long before it became a fashionable artistic movement. But now with the advent of computers and keyword searching, books can be accessed with a multiplicity of approaches. The subject heading is no longer king and neither is the cataloger. May he/she rest in peace.

Notes

1. Louis P. Stuckey, "Cataloging in a Fast Food Society," *Technical Services News* (December 13, 1990) 12–15.

2. Miles Magadan Moorhead, *Dumb Cataloger Jokes* (Frost Proof, FL: Orange Skin Press, 1986).

3. Miles Magadan Moorhead, *Theories on the Origin of Catalogers* (Frost Proof, FL: Orange Skin Press, 1989), p. 2.

4. Leo Louis Hanks, *101 Uses of a Dead Cataloger and 99 Uses of an Obsolete Cataloger* (Cleveland: Gallows Publications, Inc., 1991), p. 17.

5. William Welford Wellington, "The Death of the Original Cataloger," *Library Underground Newsletter* (September 12, 1991) 23.

6. *Ibid.*, 25.

7. Zoe Shillington, "Subject Headings I Would Have Welcomed," *The Irrepressible Librarian* (June 1990) 41.

YOUTH SERVICES

My daughter was not yelling. She was exercising her First Amendment rights.

Are youth services necessary?

The conventional wisdom of course is that the future of libraries in America rests with our children, but it can also be said that the future of anything rests with our children. That is a rather sobering thought unless you are in the entertainment industry. Humphrey Springett put it rather well in his book *Impending Doom: The Coming Cultural Ice Age:* "These are dark days for literacy. SAT scores keep plummeting and adult illiteracy rates are climbing. Young people are no longer print oriented. They are simply not developing the skills necessary to comprehend, much less, create anything with any verbal complexity. Where past great civilizations may have eroded from ecological catastrophes, ours is threatened more by the laxity induced by an addiction to entertainment. Our future ability to think, do research, and even to communicate is in great danger, and cultural institutions such as museums, galleries, and libraries will become more and more irrelevant to our increasingly less sophisticated citizenry."[1]

Does that mean that the situation is hopeless?

Dr. Stringfellow Cherrington, director of the Hutchinson Foundation for Great Literature, has warned us in an article entitled *The Trivialization of the American Library* that there is a growing tendency among librarians not only to accept this cultural debasement but to actively participate in it. Cherrington asks: "How else do you explain the proliferation of entertainment resources in the library? The current strategy of many librarians is obviously to 'go with the flow.' They feel that if young people really want videogames over books, then they must give them what they want or risk rejection."[2]

Does this philosophy spell doom for youth librarianship as we know it?

At least this philosophy recognizes the importance of getting young people interested in the library and trying to mold lifelong supporters out of them. This is preferable to the more extreme position that public libraries should abandon children's librarianship altogether. Consider the deplorable comments of Edwin A. Glover, a high profile library consultant, who was hired by a large East Coast public library to make an analysis of why the library was on the verge of financial collapse (isn't that ironic—they pay somebody $50,000 to tell them why they are broke). In his final report he wrote: "The governing board should give serious consideration to adopting a strategic plan that acknowledges the wasteful duplication in services that exists between the city's public library and its many school libraries. Economies of scale will result from the public library's full divestiture of youth services to the school district."[3] The translation of all this management babble is quite simple: "Ditch children's services because kids don't vote."

But isn't there some unfortunate truth to the view that public library governing boards need to become more politically savvy to protect and develop their institutions?

Absolutely, but abandoning children's services in this day and age is probably the worst political mistake that a library governing board could possibly make. Right now kids are very hot politically speaking. As political observer and global economist Gail Shillington has written in her article "How to Fix America's Fast Food Economy": "If you put Jesse Jackson, Bill Clinton, Dan Quayle, and Pat Robertson into a room for five hours, you will discover that they all agree on one thing and one thing only—the importance of educating our young people."[4]

The point is that there is a general consensus in America today that all our economic problems stem from one thing: Americans are stupid. Why are Americans stupid? That's easy. We're stupid because we're not learning anything in school. Our educational system is substandard.

Norman A. Halverson, in a provocative article entitled "America's Second Stupidity Crisis," compares today's situation to the Sputnik crisis of 1957. He writes, "Japan's takeover of the American automobile industry has given America the same kind of shock that it received in 1957 when the Soviet Union launched Sputnik. The fear then was that we were ripe for a military takeover by a superior foe. The fear now is that we are ripe for an economic takeover by a more industrious business competitor. In both situations we blamed our inferior position on an inadequate educational system."[5]

What does the educational reform movement mean to libraries?

It means that if we librarians were smart we'd jump on this band-wagon. The politically savvy thing to do is to position the library as an institution of learning. In fact, more than that we should be making the case that our vast network of libraries forms the very foundation that supports America's educational infrastructure.

But isn't the word "library" synonymous with the concept of educa-tion?

Yes, absolutely, but the problem lies in the fact that librarians no longer seem to want to be thought of as people who work in libraries. Too many of us prefer to be associated with "media centers," "collective memory centers," "learning materials centers," "multimedia resource facilities," and "information centers." The word "library" is apparently too old hat and is fraught with too many undesirable stereotypes. We prefer something a bit sexier.

But as Shakespeare would say, "What's in a name? A rose by any other name smells as sweet."

No, we're not just talking about a name change. We're talking about a name change that reflects a whole new purpose. Susan Saun-ders emphasizes this point in a recent *School Librarian* article entitled "Students Need School Libraries Not School Media Centers." Her main point is that "students need books much more than they need computers, games, toys, videotapes, films, puzzles, realia, and compact discs." She goes on to say that media centers are where you go to have fun rather than to learn or develop your reading skills. In her words, "the library hour of twenty years ago has become the play period of today. This has not only had a negative impact on the educa-tional performance of students, but it has also given them unfortunate expectations of what they should be able to find in their public libraries."[6]

Picking up on this theme and taking it even further is the iconoclastic Rudolph Hurd, whose article "How School Media Specialists Are Killing Librarianship" created a minitempest in the library world last year. Besides calling them "traitors" to the library profession, Hurd accuses media specialists of being the moral equivalent of educational drug dealers. He writes, "Historians will not be kind to the following ten occupational groups when they go hunting for the reasons behind the decline and fall of American civilization:

THE 10 OCCUPATIONAL GROUPS THAT WILL CAUSE THE DECLINE AND FALL OF OUR AMERICAN CIVILIZATION

1. Television talk show hosts
2. Television game show hosts
3. Liposuction technicians
4. Chiropractors
5. Junk bond salesmen
6. Authors of fad diet books
7. Pet psychiatrists
8. Las Vegas night club performers who use animals in their acts
9. Fitness video celebrities
10. School media specialists."

Hurd is confident that historians "will discover that by luring children away from books and into the multimedia world of tapes and discs, school media specialists will have killed more young brain cells than all the cocaine, heroin, hashish, and marijuana dealers put together."[7]

Dr. Donna Shalimar, author of the thought provoking and bestselling book *Betrayed by Our Schools*, obviously agrees with Hurd. She writes, "Instead of nurturing an appreciation and love for fine writing, our school media specialists have done everything they could possibly think of to dissociate themselves from books, as though the mere thought of the word would drive children away."[8]

With the new national emphasis on "back to basics" in education won't libraries revert to a more traditional approach to youth services?

There will be a lot of lip service to that effect, but whether this will translate into action is highly doubtful. Children and teenagers simply do not fit in compatibly with the hurried and superficial lifestyle of our entertainment age.

For example, let's talk about the Schoo family. In many respects they are the representative American family of the 90s. You remember that fun couple, David and Sharon Schoo. They're the husband and wife team who jetted off to Acapulco for a much deserved nine day Christmas vacation. Nothing wrong with that until it was discovered that they had left their two daughters—Nicole, 9, and Dianna, 4—home alone back in St. Charles, Illinois. The girls were rescued by a neighbor when a smoke alarm went off. Fortunately, the youngsters survived the ordeal, but the really interesting part of the story was the outrage of the American people and the American media toward David and Sharon Schoo. Overnight they became national villains, a designation they certainly deserved, but really, I've never seen so many glass housed people throwing stones in my life. The Schoos are nothing more than an extreme case of the epidemic of child neglect that has been sweeping America. It's an epidemic that begins and ends with television.

You can't really seriously suggest that the Schoos are a typical American family?

In his book *Why America Hates Kids,* Jonathan Mortimer makes the highly provocative point that the parents of the 70s, 80s, and 90s had as their parenting model not their own mothers and fathers but the mothers and fathers that they watched on television—Ward and June Cleaver, Ozzie and Harriet Nelson, and Rob and Laura Petrie, among others. These parents were wise, witty and sympathetic, but stern when they had to be, and always very effective. Sure, Beaver, Wally, Ricky, and David all had their problems but there was nothing that Mom or Dad couldn't fix.

Mortimer poses the question: "What happens when young people grow up with these idealized images of parenthood and then are subjected to the real things?"[9] Indeed, what happens when your kids simply don't respond like Wally and Beaver? According to Mortimer there's a natural tendency on the part of the parents to give up and say,

"Hey, kid, you won't listen to me. Then you better watch Cliff Huxtable on television." He goes on to write, "The real harm of all the family comedy shows that have been a part of our national consciousness for the last thirty years is that they have given the very false impression that parenting is a fairly quick and easy task."[10]

Nothing could be more incorrect. The reality, of course, is that parenting is the most difficult, most frustrating, and most time intensive task that anyone could ever undertake. And when parents discover this they don't want any part of it. In fact they grow to resent their own children, and like the Schoos they take off and do their own thing and leave the kids in front of the tube to watch, guess what—idyllic family comedies. It's a vicious cycle.

Of course most parents are not as blatant as the Schoos. Most parents hide behind that great guilt relaxing maxim, "It's not the quantity of time that you spend with your children that's important, it's the quality of time that counts." They would never leave the kids alone in front of the television for nine days like the Schoos did, but nine *hours* is very normal. The difference is in degree, not kind.

What's all this got to do with librarianship?

It's the same syndrome. We librarians like the concept of serving children (doing story hours, providing reader's advisory advice to both parents and children, and working hard to develop reading skills) far more than the actual reality of serving children (the noise, the tears, and the chaos). So what do we do, we satiate them with toys, films, videotapes, and PacMan games.

Why is the reality of children's librarianship so grim?

Because, let's face it, being a kid is grim. Although we like to think of childhood in the happiest of Hallmark terms, the reality is something quite different. Throughout history children have been abused and misused, and great authors from Charles Dickens to Jonathan Kozol have graphically portrayed this reality. Even Huckleberry Finn, that symbol of youthful insouciance, was an abused child. His pap was a violent, abusive alcoholic.

In a book entitled *Alien on an Alien Planet,* psychologist Dr. Hillary M. Bertleson writes, "Most adults have totally blocked out their childhood, which makes it very difficult for them to understand what it is like to be a child today."[11] To regain that feeling of being a young child, Bertleson recommends that adults undertake the following 13 step envisioning exercise:

TO FEEL LIKE A YOUNG CHILD, PRETEND THAT . . .

1. One day after traveling for nine months in a very small oval shaped spaceship you suddenly land with a thud on an alien planet where 93 percent of the people are as tall as Wilt Chamberlain.

2. You have a great deal of difficulty understanding or speaking the language of these very tall people.

3. These very tall people have a great deal of difficulty understanding you.

4. Whenever you whine or cry because these very tall people cannot understand you, you are plunked down in front of a television and are forced to watch a program in which a very tall and very boring man named Mr. Rogers is constantly changing his sweater and shoes.

5. You discover that you are incontinent and that you drool a lot.

6. You are constantly being yelled at by these very tall people for being incontinent and for drooling too much.

7. Many of these very tall people live with furry, four-legged animals.

8. Many of these four legged "pets" have sharp teeth.

9. Your own teeth are not very sharp, which makes it very difficult to eat the food that these very tall people feed you.

10. You are constantly being yelled at by these very tall people for not eating all of your food.

11. You are not able to walk and run very quickly or efficiently but you are expected to keep up with these very tall people who all seem to be very good walkers and runners.

12. You find it very difficult to sit on the furniture that these very tall people use and so you sit on the floor a lot and are consequently called a "rug rat."

13. You get slapped and yelled at by these very tall people for doing the very same things that they do—turning on the kitchen stove, lighting matches, opening the refrigerator, and putting the car in drive.[12]

Bertleson's point is that there is a great deal of grimness and violence in the process of what she calls "the initiation into the human race." Despite what all the greeting cards say, the business of becoming a human being is terribly risky. You start out as a fetus and your first danger is abortion. If you're not aborted, you are still susceptible to a mother's diseases—AIDS, alcoholism, and drug addiction, to name a few. What did you do to deserve that? Then there is the abrupt ejection from your mother's womb into the bright lights of your father's camcorder. And then of course there is the rather terrifying acculturation to the new environment, an environment where you, the child, are always completely vulnerable.

No one would ever deny that infancy and toddlerhood are difficult stages to survive, but things do get better after the terrible two's don't they?

Obviously the feeling of being an alien on an alien planet begins to fade by the third year, but really the years between three and five are not exactly edenic. Consider these indignities as put forth by the bestselling author Mary Jo Conover, America's "tell it like it is" homemaker:

THE INDIGNITIES OF THE PRESCHOOL YEARS

1. Getting toilet trained by a committee of grossed out parents, siblings, and babysitters.

2. Getting a sweater for Christmas that looks just like the one that Mr. Rogers wears.

3. Wearing mittens with metal clips that get very cold in chilly, wet weather.

4. Getting yelled at for throwing up on the family room barcalounger after being forced to eat your Aunt Bertie's rancid jello salad.

5. Getting yelled at for bleeding on the living room carpet after being attacked by Hank, your Uncle Leo's predatory pit bull.

6. Being hugged by your Grandma Nellie whose perfume smells like a cat that's been dead for three days.

7. Getting a quarter from your Grandpa Henry who makes it seem like he just gave you the Trump fortune.

8. Walking around with the peas that you secretly stuffed into your pocket so that you wouldn't have to eat them.

9. Having your parents spell words that you're not supposed to hear.

10. Having your father monopolize your Lego set because according to him his parents couldn't afford to buy him one when he was your age.[13]

Enough already! Certainly the elementary school years are the most wonderful time in a child's life, aren't they?

Not according to the research data of child psychologist Dr. Susan Sterling Sutherland, who conducted open-ended interviews with over 2,000 elementary school children. According to her findings, school age children have more bad things to say about their lives than good things:

TEN COMPLAINTS THAT THE AVERAGE ELEMENTARY SCHOOL CHILD HAS ABOUT LIFE

1. Roger Rabbit cartoons are not piped into the school cafeteria.

2. Mom still thinks I get a kick out of Mr. Rogers.

3. Christmas only comes once a year.

4. It is very difficult to remember the name of Mom's latest boyfriend.

5. Disneyland is only open 17 hours a day.

6. Dad's girlfriend can never remember my name.

7. My Dad thinks that just because he spends $45 on a Nintendo game that he should be allowed to play with it whenever he comes for a visit.

8. I'm not allowed to take off from school on my birthday.

9. Most teachers do not allow book reports to be done on *Where's Waldo* books.

10. The Grand Canyon has not been converted to a "Great America" type theme park.[14]

Sorry to say, but by the time the child is firmly ensconced in elementary school he or she has weathered a lot—sibling rivalries, separation and divorce, substantial neglect, probable abuse, possible molestation, varying degrees of poverty, and exposure to a veritable pantheon of antiheroes — Madonna, Prince, Axl Rose, and, yes, even the drunken, unruly Roger Rabbit.

But the defining characteristic of American children is their exposure to television. It's not so much the programs that are the problem here. It's the advertising that corrupts children and turns them into greedy little materialists who grow up thinking that the meaning of life resides inside an amusement park, a movie theater, a video game machine, or a box of sugary breakfast cereal. Breakfast cereal, by the way, is the child's first narcotic experience, and it is what leads older children to experiment with other, more potent types of drugs like Twinkies, Hohos, and those strawberry/coconut cakes with the sticky creme filling.

Enough about children! Why is the life of the children's librarian so grim?

In her article "Runny Noses and No Respect," Nancy Torkelsen, children's librarian at the Edgarville (Idaho) Public Library, identifies the three main sources of frustration in the lives of children's librarians:

1. *Kids.* The only thing worse than being a kid is working with kids. Kids are obstreperous, cantankerous and noisy, and they ask idiotic questions. They fall down stairs, peel property stickers off library books, demand money back when they return books early, drool on fabric chairs, and clog up library toilets with play dough. They also sneeze on you, barf on you, and pee on you, but one thing they never do is say "thank you," which is something that people working in adult services get a lot of.

2. *Librarians.* Library administrators, adult services librarians, computer techies, catalogers, and acquisitions librarians have no respect for children's librarians. Even though they would never want to get within fifty feet of the children's area, these librarians see it as a kind of glorified toy department where a lot of time is spent finger painting, doing crafts, and getting hugs. In fact many adult services librarians feel that children's librarians should be paid less because all they do is play all day. This illusion is also harbored by administrators who feel that children's librarianship

(because it is so much fun) is not a good preparation for an administrative career.

This sense of disdain for children's librarians reflects a very odd pecking order in the entire industry of education: Professors who teach graduate students look down upon professors who teach undergraduates who look down upon high school teachers who look down upon junior high school teachers who look down upon middle school teachers who look down upon primary school teachers who look down upon kindergarten teachers who look down upon nursery school teachers who look down upon day care attendants who look down upon mothers who stay home and take care of their babies. The irony of this pattern of disrespect is that psychologists tell us that the most important period in a person's life is the first three years.

3. *Parents.* By far the parents are a children's librarian's biggest source of frustration. They are of two types: indifferent, and involved. Oddly enough, the indifferent parent is often the lesser of the two evils. This is the parent who abandons the kid in the children's library and goes off browsing in the adult library, goes shopping, goes to work, goes back home, or takes a trip to Acapulco. There is this growing trend among parents that they are not responsible for their children once those children enter a library or a school. The child is now the responsibility of the staff. That's why parents pay taxes. So they can dump their children on overworked and underpaid children's librarians. That way, if a kid sticks his finger in an electrical outlet and electrocutes himself or slides down a stairway banister and breaks his neck it's the librarian's fault.

As bad as this sounds, the involved parent is often a bigger problem. This is because the involved parent is usually a very intense human being and very intense human beings have a tendency to create tension which is of course why they are called inTENSE. Involved parents meddle, complain, berate, and demand.[15]

Wait a minute, what's wrong with being concerned about your child?

There's a big difference between the concerned parent and the intense parent. The concerned parent has the child's best interest at heart. This is not always the case with the intense parent who more often than not places his or her own ego needs above the needs of the child. Florence Kinsley has offered this guide to be able to recognize an intense parent:

YOU KNOW A PARENT IS INTENSE WHEN HE/SHE SAYS...

1. Do you have anything more intellectually challenging than Dr. Seuss for little Tina? After all, she'll be two next week.

2. Please do not berate Judith for sliding down the banister. Her ballet teacher thinks she will be an Olympic gymnastics champion, and this is good training for her.

3. I know that Troy shouldn't have put his gum in the computer terminal, but after all, he is only three, and that means he's in his experimental phase.

4. Don't you think that Cinderella is an inappropriate book for Story Hour. It's so dreadfully sexist.

5. Yes, I know that Tina knocked over your Halloween display. I watched her do it. It's all right. Remember, she's four. She's working through her discovery phase.

6. So what if Debbie has forty-seven books overdue? There's no child in this community who has a better use for them than her.

7. Although Jonathan is only three he belongs in the five year old crafts class because he's so gifted. Yesterday he created the most wonderful abstract painting with spaghetti sauce and bubblegum on a paper plate. I have named it "A Study in Ambiguity."

8. Yes, I know that little Leo is disruptive in Story Hour, but that's because he's bored. He has a genius level intellect. You need to give him learning opportunities that are more cerebrally oriented than a felt board presentation of *Little Red Riding Hood.* Have you ever thought about doing a finger puppet play of the dagger scene in *Macbeth?*

9. What if Shawn and Heather have been playing hide-and-go-seek in the nonfiction area? You wouldn't want me to put them in one of those awful leashes would you?

10. Hillary is not yelling, she's exercising her First Amendment rights!

11. I know that Eddie stabbed Dewey, the library hamster, with a pencil, but you have to remember that Eddie is only five years old. He's in the middle of his inquiry stage.

12. Of course Henry is throwing books around. He's angry. Your mediocre collection has nothing that speaks to his unique interests in the area of electrical engineering.

13. You're upset that Sherry had a bathroom accident in your Story Hour? Are you anal retentive or something?[16]

Are there any good things about working in the children's department?

Yes, Cody Ann Coplestand identifies three. She writes, "First, you get to read juvie fiction, play with kids' toys, and watch children's movies without anyone thinking you're weird. Second, you tend to get left alone by administrators, most of whom would rather walk on hot coals than get near our beastly little patrons and their horrid little parents. Third, you can wear tee shirts and jeans to work because everybody thinks all you do is play with paint and glue."[17]

How about burnout? Is it a problem for children's librarians?

Yes, according to Sandra Blanchard of the Stoneman (Wyoming) Public Library, burnout is a problem. As you might expect it is caused far more by working with parents than by working with kids, and it usually manifests itself in physical symptoms such as hives, upset stomachs, and headaches.[18]

A far greater problem for children's librarians, however, is what Dr. Sandford Higgins calls DIWJB syndrome. This stands for "Dysfunctional Identification With Juvenile Behavior" and it's also often found among preschool, kindergarten, and primary teachers. In layman's terms it is more commonly known as a reversion to childhood. After doing extensive research among children's librarians, Dr. Higgins has identified the following sixteen warning signs of DIWJB syndrome:

SIXTEEN WARNING SIGNS THAT A CHILDREN'S LIBRARIAN MAY BE REVERTING TO CHILDHOOD

1. Begins talking to everyone through finger puppets.
2. Likes to take naps after doing afternoon story hours.
3. Wants smiley stickers placed on his or her yearly performance evaluation.
4. Can easily be bribed with pieces of candy.
5. Won't work on Saturday mornings because of conflict with television cartoon shows.
6. Says, "I'd like you to meet Tinkerbelle, she's the newest member of our Youth Advisory Board."
7. Often can be heard humming "Rubber Duckie."
8. Does interdepartmental memoranda in crayon.
9. Carries the official ALA stuffed Paddington Bear everywhere.

10. Joins Big Bird's fan club.

11. Gets the ALA READ poster of Miss Piggy framed for the office wall.

12. Begins dressing like a walrus to do sleepy-time story hour.

13. Reads *Goodnight Moon* to spouse every night at bedtime.

14. Begins packing lunch in a Donald Duck lunch box.

15. Removes furniture from children's department office and replaces it with bean bag chairs.

16. Shows up at the staff lingerie party and asks if they have any flannel pajamas with feet for sale.[19]

What can be done to help the children's librarian who has reverted to juvenile behavior?

More than anything, according to Dr. Higgins, the children's librarian suffering from a reversion malady needs constant exposure to the adult world. For instance, when you sit down with him or her to eat lunch do not talk about the latest Walt Disney movie or Judy Blume book. Talk about adult things like, you know, global warming, the ozone layer, the unstable political environment in Eastern Europe, the health care crisis, the stock market, and what's been happening with the Royal Family. Also, if you're an adult services librarian, recommend a good adult novel to your suffering colleague, and don't forget to include this person in your adult social plans. Bring him or her along to the next staff Happy Hour attitude adjustment session or even to a blasted Tupperware party for that matter because there is absolutely nothing better than a Tupperware party to bring someone back to reality.[20]

What can children's librarians do to garner more support for their services?

This is easy. If a children's librarian wants to enhance his or her department all he has to do is knock on the director's door and say, "Hey, if you want to increase adult usage in your library, take money out of adult services and give it to me in children's!"

Say what? I don't get it.

Every public library director wants to increase the library's patron base. We all want to turn non–library users into users, but it's not simply a matter of having the best of intentions. It actually has more to do with following the right strategy. Nine times out of ten when we say we want to bring more people into the library we are talking about the hordes of adults who often stop using the library right after they get their high school diploma or their college degree.

So what do we do? We work feverishly to develop and enhance adult programs and adult collections in a valiant attempt to attract these people. Does it ever work? Only rarely and even in those exceptional cases the gains are minimal. If adults do not have the library habit, a special program on how to wrap Christmas presents or a guest lecture on the films and writings of Woody Allen will simply not do the trick, nor will fancy flyers, spiffy annual reports, creative press releases, or luncheon speeches to the Rotary Club.

You can do all the wonderfully creative things that the people who write books on adult programming and public relations recommend but it won't make a bit of difference because none of those things pack the punch required to knock people out of old habits and into new ones. Don't despair, however, because there is a dead solid perfect way to accomplish what you're after. It's dead solid perfect, that is, if your library is not in Sun City, Arizona, or in an elder-care facility.

If you want to increase your adult user base, then take money out of adult services and put it into children's. Don't worry. There is method to this madness. Kids are the greatest public relations tool that public libraries have, because they serve as a catalyst in getting their mothers, fathers, aunts, uncles, grandparents, and babysitters into the library.

The harsh reality of life is that we do things for our children that we will do for nobody else. Consider this: I am the world's biggest Notre Dame football fan. I can tell you the first, last, and middle names of the famous Four Horseman backfield, the score of the 1925 Rose Bowl game against Stanford, and the career record of every head coach ever hired by the Fighting Irish. The only thing that could keep me away from the television on Notre Dame football Saturdays would be, well, a fourth grade band concert. That's right, in the last thirty years the only time I ever missed a Notre Dame football game was because of a fourth grade band concert.

Now, why did I go to the concert? Was it because I love to hear John Philip Sousa music played by ten year olds? Of course not. It was because my son, Michael, the world's greatest third trumpet player, was a member of this elite group of musicians. The fact of the matter is that we adults do things for our kids that we would never, ever dream of doing on our own. Consider the list of things I have done for my children over the past twenty-one years:

1. Backtracked 160 miles on a hot August afternoon on Interstate 40 in Oklahoma to search for a raggedy Kermit the Frog hand puppet that my son "accidently" dropped out the window.

2. Got into a fist fight with a 250 pound man who called my son a "wimp" after he struck out with the bases loaded in a Little League baseball game.

3. Crawled into the crawlspace under my house to retrieve a renegade hamster named Max.

4. Held a formal funeral (with prayers, incense, and holy water) for Max in my backyard shortly after his corpse was found under the family room sofa.

5. Fished yellow play dough out of the toilet of my master bathroom.

6. Ate a piece of green and red Rice Krispie Treat for my Christmas dinner dessert.

7. Put the finishing touches on a flour dough map of the Mississippi River Basin at 3:00 A.M.

8. Delivered newspapers in a driving rain at 5:30 A.M. on New Year's morning.

9. Attended the world's worst theatrical production of "The Three Little Pigs" and maintained an appreciative smile throughout the performance.

10. Ate three boxes of Fruity Yummy Mummy cereal so that my kid could get the boxtops he needed to get the complete Fruity Yummy Mummy figurine set.

11. Stood in line at Disneyland for two hours for a ride (Space Mountain) that made me throw up.

12. Bought 27 pounds of peanut brittle so that my son could meet his Cub Scout quota.

That's why children's services should be a public library's number one priority. Children bring parents to the library. There is, for example, nothing more persuasive than a three year old little girl who wants to go to Story Hour. Smart librarians use that three year old as bait to catch the parents, and once the parents are caught I am very confident that they will find much of interest in the library.

Getting them in the door—that's the key. For that reason we should be more concerned with the question, "What can children do for us?" than "What can we do for children?"

What about the young adult librarian? Does he or she have a future?

The question is better phrased, "Do young adults have a future?" That's the real key. It's just like the relationship between alligators and the people who hunt alligators. If the alligators become extinct, the people who hunt them are going to be out of business.

You can't possibly be suggesting that young adults are dying at an alarming rate?

No, they're not dying. They just don't exist anymore. In our society you're either a child or an adult. Today's world is a place where you're forced to grow up fast. "Latchkey kids," "crack cocaine," "abortion on demand," "birth control pills," "safe sex," "cable television," "X-rated video"—these are terms that weren't even in our vocabulary thirty years ago when we were going to high school, but now they're a routine part of the everyday lives of our young people. In our day, acne was the big medical issue; now it's AIDS. This means that today kids have to grow up right away. There's no time for a leisurely transition. If you doubt this, check out a seventh grade classroom sometime. The girls are all dressed like Madonna.

But doesn't this situation scream out for the need for more services for teenagers, not less?

Obviously, but if kids are bad, teenagers are horrific. No one wants to have teenagers around. That's why I think society is trying to eliminate the concept of the young adult. We think that by eliminating the concept that we can eliminate the reality that teenagers really do inhabit this planet.

What is so wrong with teenagers?

Four things: (1) they think they know everything, (2) they think that everyone else is stupid, (3) they try to make themselves look as ugly as possible, and (4) they seem to be biologically incapable of communicating with adults.

What kind of librarian ends up working in young adult services?

First of all, you have to remember that there are at last count only 93 young adult librarians left in America, and you'd have to guess that 47 percent of these people got into young adult librarianship because they couldn't get a job anywhere else. The other 53 percent are probably the most dedicated people in the library profession. They truly believe that they have a calling to help these young people integrate into the real world by providing them with the books and information that will help them make wise decisions when confronted with the serious issues that will test their maturity.

What are the hazards of working in young adult services?

According to Dr. Ellen H. Beasley of the Middlecenter Institute of Library Studies, the young adult librarian runs a real risk of trying to present him or herself as being hip in the eyes of the teenager. Many young adult librarians mistakenly think that in order to communicate with young adults you have to speak their language, wear their clothes, dance their dances, listen to their music, and eat their food. This, of course, is a fatal mistake that always makes the librarian look not only foolish but, ironically enough, about as unhip as you could possibly be.

In Dr. Beasley's words, "What is more pathetic than a forty-five year old librarian with a mohawk hairdo boogeying to the strains of Guns and Roses?"[21]

This sentiment is seconded by Dorothy Quinlan, head of Young Adult Services for the Grasley (Maine) Public Library in an article entitled "Why Young Adults Look Ugly." In the article Quinlan points out that teenagers are ugly for three basic reasons: (1) acne, (2) their developing body parts don't fit together quite right, and (3) they *want* to look ugly in order to distinguish themselves from everyone older and younger than they are. They want to establish their own identity by creating their own unique "look," and that accounts for their weird hairdos, outlandish earrings, holey clothes, and ugly work boots. It is, therefore, supremely insulting to them to have an adult try to ape this "look."[22]

How can you tell if your young adult librarian is trying to achieve teen hipness?

Quinlan says that there are ten definite warning signs:

TEN SURE SIGNS THAT A YOUNG ADULT LIBRARIAN IS TRYING TO BE HIP

1. Can be seen at the shopping mall running up the down escalator.
2. Stops at 7-Eleven every night after work to play the video-game machines and hang around the phone booth.
3. Starts experimenting with purple hair dye.
4. Looks up the side effects of inhaling white-out.
5. Starts exposing the elastic band of his/her jockey shorts.
6. Gets rollerblades for Christmas.
7. Begins to use the word "like" in place of the word "say" (e.g., "I'm like, 'You can't expect me to work every Saturday'").
8. Begins to use the word "like" in place of the word "thinking" (e.g., "I'm like I can't believe this is happening to me").
9. Starts quoting Madonna in staff meetings.
10. Begins referring to humankind as "dudes" and "du-dettes."[23]

What is the best remedy for a "hip" YA librarian?

A six month transfer to cataloging.

Notes

1. Humphrey Springett, *Impending Doom: The Coming Cultural Ice Age* (Iowa City: Educational Concepts, Inc., 1990), p. 7.

2. Stringfellow Cherrington, *The Trivialization of the American Library* (Philadelphia: Hutchinson Foundation Publications, 1991), p. 33.

3. Edwin Aldrich Glover, "Report on a Study of the H.W. Bilkington Memorial Library" (1989), p. 87.

4. Gail Shillington, "How to Fix America's Fast Food Economy," *The Journal of Economic Reform in America* (April 1992) 87.

5. Norman Anthony Halverson, "America's Second Stupidity Crisis," *The Journal of Contemporary Educational Thought* (spring 1989) 34.

6. Susan Saunders, "Students Need School Libraries Not School Media Centers," *School Librarian* (September 1990) 81.

7. Rudolph Hurd, "How School Media Specialists Are Killing Librarianship," *The Journal of Library Philosophy* (winter 1990) 113–114.

8. Donna Shalimar, *Betrayed by Our Schools* (Palo Alto: The Severinson Institute Press, 1991), p. 79.

9. Jonathan Applebody Mortimer, *Why America Hates Kids* (Dallas: Institute for the Study of Young People, 1992), p. 223.

10. *Ibid.*, p. 224.

11. Hillary M. Bertleson, *Alien on an Alien Planet* (Kansas City: Red Brick Press, 1988), p. 231.

12. *Ibid.*, pp. 232–233.

13. Mary Jo Conover, *Tripping Over the Tricycle* (New York: Masters and Masters, 1990), pp. 73–74.

14. Susan Sterling Sutherland, "Life Perspectives of School Age Children," *Primary School Monthly* (February 1986) 34–35.

15. Nancy Torkelsen, "Runny Noses and No Respect," *Youth Services Weekly Hotline* (March 12, 1988) 3–5.

16. Florence Kinsley, "Problem Parents—An Identification Guide," *Public Library Issues Quarterly* (winter 1990) 14–15.

17. Cody Ann Coplestand, "Life in the Library Toy Department," *The Contemporary Librarian* (September 1987) 347.

18. Sandra Blanchard, "Burnout Is More Than a Reference Problem," *Library World* (October 1990) 77.

19. Sandford Higgins, "The Symptons of D.I.W.J.B. Syndrome," *The Contemporary Librarian* (June 1991) 157–159.

20. *Ibid.*, 163.

21. Ellen H. Beasley, "Communicating with Teenage Patrons," *The Young Adult Librarian Newsletter* (May 15, 1991) 7.

22. Dorothy Quinlan, "Why Young Adults Look Ugly," *The Irrepressible Librarian* (August 1991) 15.

23. *Ibid.*, 16–17.

MANAGEMENT

Last year Mrs. Roberts searched for excellence. This year she's searching for her inner child.

Is management really necessary?

Yes because human beings are unfortunately not very perfect. They can be selfish, lazy, greedy, close-minded, cruel, petty, impersonal, and unwilling to cooperate with each other. In any organization there needs to be someone who has responsibility for setting goals and getting everybody working together to accomplish those goals.

What is the first law of library management?

Figure out why your library exists and what it should be doing.

What is the second law of library management?

Hire the right people to do it.

What is the third law of library management?

Let those people do it with a minimum of interference.

What is the fourth law of library management?

Hire fewer managers than you really need.

Explain the fourth law.

The most efficiently run libraries are those in which there are so few managers that they do not have time to do "management things." If you are understaffed with managers you increase the probability that your managers will actually manage and decrease the chances that they will do management things.

What is the difference between managing and doing management things?

Managing consists of hiring the right people, organizing them, defining their respective roles, and removing obstacles from their path so that they can do the work of the library with as little interference as possible. Doing management things consists of writing reports, conducting audits, drawing up goals and objectives, gathering statistics, making lists, implementing morale programs, making long range plans, putting together public relations campaigns, developing strategic plans, implementing quality assurance programs, holding workshops, seminars, and retreats, making evaluations, monitoring cost effectiveness, measuring key indicators, running cost-benefit analyses, producing memoranda, writing policy statements, putting together procedure manuals, developing option packages, diagnosing the organizational climate, and surveying the constituency base.

To define it another way, when you manage you remove obstacles from the working lives of your employees. You blast through the bureaucracy and allow your employees to do the work that they are trained to do. But when you do management things you put obstacles in their way by giving them unnecessary paperwork to do, unproductive meetings to attend, and extra layers of bureaucracy to maneuver through.

A good example of a "management thing" can be found in an article entitled "Measuring Reference Productivity" by Aaron Jasperson. The gist of the article is that after tinkering for over three years with various productivity formulae, Jasperson came up with something called the "Q Factor" to measure reference output.[1] What the "Q" stands for is anybody's guess but one thing that it most assuredly does not stand for is "Quick" because this is a very complicated mathematical process that forces the reference librarian to determine (for statistical purposes) a difficulty level, a usefulness index, and a patron satisfaction rating for each reference question that he or she answers.

The irony of the article is that in it Jasperson unwittingly illustrates just how nonproductive his productivity index really is. If you analyze his data closely you notice that after he implemented the Q Factor measurement technique in his reference department, the number of reference questions answered decreased by almost 17 percent. The obvious conclusion to make from this is that Jasperson's librarians were so busy inputting Q Factor data into their computers that they did not have as much time to spend helping patrons. This is a perfect example of how service to the public is hurt when staff members are involved in doing management things. It is bad enough when managers do management things but when they require rank and file employees to do management things the impact is doubly bad.

What are the telltale signs that your organization is too involved with doing management things?

Jonathan N. Yardley, professor of management science at the Farmington School of Library and Information Studies, provides the following list of activities that would signify an overly bureaucratic library:

NINE SIGNS THAT YOUR LIBRARY
HAS BECOME TOO BUREAUCRATIC

1. Your janitor comes to see you about "an urgent need for new equipment," and instead of asking for a new vacuum cleaner or floor buffer he requests a personal computer to prepare the weekly reports that the head of library maintenance has assigned him to do.

2. You ask your head of Circulation for a copy of her departmental goals and objectives and she says, "Which ones — our twenty-five-year long-range strategic goals, our five-year midrange strategic goals, our one-year shortrange strategic goals, our quarterly goals, our monthly goals, or our weekly goals?"

3. When you wander into the Children's Room you notice a sign on the service counter that says "BE BACK IN FOUR HOURS." Upon investigation you discover that all three of your children's librarians are down in the library's program room attending a "Quality Circle" meeting where the main topic of conversation is written on the blackboard: "How Can We Improve Service to the Public?"

4. Your head of Cataloging requests permission to spend $5,000 to hire a management consultant to find out why the cataloging budget has been overspent three years in a row.

5. Your assistant director announces that he is launching a new project called "Vision 2100." He explains that when finished, this long range strategic plan will identify the library's needs into the year 2100 and beyond.

6. Your business manager drops the audit report that he has

been working on for two months on your desk. You notice that the title on the cover sheet is "Hand Dryers vs. Paper Towels: A Comparative Cost Analysis."

7. You get a bill for $3,000 from a local recording studio. Further checking indicates that your Reference Department has recorded its annual report on cassette tape in the form of a rap song entitled, "We're the Reference Staff with the Baddest Stats."

8. Down in the Periodicals Room you notice that one of your librarians is very busy making a list of the names and dates of all the magazines that have been checked out of the closed stacks in the previous two hours. When you ask the purpose of the list, he just shrugs his shoulders and says, "It's just something we've always done around here."

9. Your personnel director sends around a sign-up sheet asking for eight volunteers to serve as a "focus group" that will make recommendations on what policy the administration should adopt with regard to brown bag lunches that are left in the staff room refrigerator for more than a week.[2]

What can a library director do to insure that his or her employees are not involved in doing management things?

Two things: (1) don't hire a lot of managers, supervisors, coordinators, and administrators, and (2) keep those that you do hire busy and out of offices. For instance, if you feel you must have a head of Reference, make sure that person spends at least three-quarters of his or her time out at the Reference Desk working right alongside the librarians. Not only does this improve services, it sets a good example for everybody else, and it frees the supervisor from the temptation of doing management things.

Helen H. Hunter, who wrote the article "The Library Without Offices," feels so strongly about this point that she designed her new 150,000 square foot library without one office. Hunter writes, "Offices do weird things to people."[3] She then goes on to describe and enumerate seven case studies illustrating her point. Among the most interesting of these were the stories of Fred Freeland and Linda Ferguson:

Fred's Story. Fred Freeland was one of those people who had gotten interested in librarianship as a career after working as a page in the Oakdale Public Library during his four years of high school. In fact he continued to work at the library for five more years as a part-time reference aide while commuting to the state university where he received a B.A. in history and then an M.L.S. After graduate school, Fred was hired by Oakdale Public as a full-time reference librarian and ten years later he was promoted to Reference head when Rosemary Ragsdale retired. Fred was the logical choice for this job. While never very exciting, he was always steady, loyal, dependable, and cooperative. He was also deeply involved in the community. Fred and his wife were lay ministers in the Dayspring Methodist Church, and twice Fred chaired the annual fundraising campaign for the Oakdale United Way.

Fred changed, however, when he moved into Rosemary's job. Some people said that it was the newfound power of the position; others felt it had something to do with the actual office that Fred moved into, and, in truth, his glass walled office was rather imposing. It was perched up on the library's mezzanine level, and from there Fred could keep a vigilant eye on his staff as they worked in the reference area below.

For whatever the reason, Fred became the kind of aloof and arrogant supervisor who enjoys wielding power over employees. What's worse, he decorated his office with the following signs: "RANK HAS ITS PRIVILEGES," "WHAT PART OF NO DON'T YOU UNDERSTAND," "DON'T LET YOUR STUPIDITY RUIN MY DAY," "THERE ARE NO STUPID QUESTIONS JUST STUPID PEOPLE," "MY DOOR IS ALWAYS OPEN BUT MY MIND IS NOT," "GIVE ME SOLUTIONS NOT PROBLEMS," and "OFFICE HOURS ARE FROM 9:00 TO 9:05 (MAKE APPOINTMENTS SIX WEEKS IN ADVANCE)."

Despite this change in personal style, Fred was certainly not what you would call an incompetent supervisor. Although he was more feared than respected, there were no open staff rebellions against him and the reference department continued to be fairly productive. But then things changed even more when Sandra McKenzie was hired by the library to implement a new multimillion-dollar computer system. It was not Sandra or her new computer that bothered Fred so much; it was more the fact that Sandra was given a newly remodeled office with brand new furniture. Fred was so overwhelmed by jealousy that one night after the library closed he creeped into Sandra's office on his hands and knees with a tape measure and measured the office, and when he discovered that Sandra's office was larger than his by 2.3

square feet something terribly ugly was released from Fred's inner being.

At first he tried to work within the system. He asked his director, Mrs. Farthingale that his office be expanded to reflect his position of superiority over Sandra on the organizational chart. Naturally Mrs. Farthingale politely refused, and when Fred responded with anger (he accused Mrs. Farthingale of favoring Sandra because she was a woman) Mrs. Farthingale became alarmed and suggested that Fred seek personal counseling "to work through some of his ego issues."

Fred left Farthingale's office seething with rage, a rage that was unleashed late that night when Fred took a chain saw into Sandra's office and proceeded to destroy everything in it. Unfortunately for Fred he was apprehended by building security and was subsequently fired and prosecuted. After being given a suspended sentence, Fred was directed to seek rehabilitative counseling to treat his psychological problems, and right now, two years later, Fred takes his life one day at a time as a cataloger in a small Midwestern library. But he is still psychologically unable to walk into a library office.

Linda's Story. When Linda Ferguson was 22 she made the same mistake that millions of other Americans make. She married the wrong person. At the time of course Linda thought that Ralph Ferguson represented everything that she would ever want in a man. He was tall, handsome, and articulate, and he seemed to have a great future as a commodities broker.

But Ralph was also a wife abuser, something that Linda discovered one evening — two years into their marriage — when Ralph came home after a bad day at the office and proceeded to push her onto the bedroom floor, slap the side of her head three times, and lock her in the room for four hours. It was a scene that Linda was to experience many times over the next ten years. Linda tolerated Ralph's violence because she was a very religious person and she felt that God wanted her to stay with Ralph and try to help him.

Finally, however, it got to be too much. Because of Linda's religious convictions she was unable to seek a divorce from Ralph but at least she did decide she needed to get out of the house more and start pursuing a life of her own. Unfortunately her B.A. degree in English did not qualify her for many good jobs and so she decided to go back to school and get an M.L.S. Two years later she got a job as a children's librarian at the Burlingame Public Library where she quickly became one of the most popular people on staff because of her warm and caring personality. And five years after that (the library was moving to a new main building) Linda was promoted to the position of head children's librarian.

After supervising the move of books, furniture, and equipment into the Children's Room, Linda set about the task of putting together her office. This was a labor of love because she had strong feelings about the importance of creating just the right ambience in a supervisory office. She felt strongly that certain environments invite communication while others discourage it. Warm, informal, friendly, and creative — these were the qualities that she was trying to achieve in her office decor.

After hours of moving her desk here and her shelves there, Linda finally got discouraged and decided to take a break. Nothing seemed to work the way she had envisioned. Because her office chairs were filled with books and plants, the only place to sit down was on the floor, and so Linda, both mentally and physically exhausted, sat lotus style on the carpet and began chanting a mantra to relax. Suddenly it dawned on her that this is what she wanted, an office where you sit on the floor.

So the next morning Linda had Tucker, the library janitor, move all the traditional furnishings — desk, chairs, credenzas, and tables — out of the office. She then went out to one of those import stores where they sell everything from muumuus to candleholders and (using her library furnishings allowance) bought two dozen oversized pillows from China, three incense holders from India, three hanging lamps from Sri Lanka, four brightly colored paintings from Thailand, and eight wicker plant holders from Singapore.

The resulting office resembled a kind of modified Oriental opium den (especially when all three incense holders were filled with burning incense). The bottom line, however, was that Linda had accomplished her goal — almost immediately her office became a mecca for people who wanted to talk or just to hang out. First the rank and file staff gravitated to it during their breaks, then teenagers from the library's YA center began to use it as a place to hold their rap sessions, and finally the homeless found their way down there and used it as a relaxing place to catch some z's. Linda had gone from being a children's librarian to being a mother earth figure.

A psychologist, of course, would probably theorize that Linda was really creating a home away from home. But who could blame her? The

more Linda blossomed on her own, the more her husband began to resent her. Consequently the abuse intensified, and eventually Linda
started living in her office. First a microwave appeared, then a refrigerator, and finally a sleeping bag.

The library director, Jack Kemperson, was not oblivious to what
was going on, but how could he stop it? Linda, even though she was
no longer functioning as a children's services supervisor or even a
librarian, was providing a very popular community service. He could
no more tell her to clean out the office than he could tell Mother
Theresa to move her hospital to another town. But it turned out that
Kemperson didn't need to. Late one night someone knocked over an
incense holder and several of the pillows ignited. The result was a
rather serious fire ($3 million worth of damage) that gutted the base-
ment floor of the library and caused the cessation of all library services
for six months. When the library was finally rebuilt, Linda was told to
arrange her office in a standard, businesslike fashion. One month later,
unable to deal with the reality of sitting on a chair with four legs, she
quit her job, divorced her husband, and opened up a shelter for abused
wives and children.[4]

What is the best way to motivate employees?
I go along with Philip Hargrove who in his new book *Money Talks*
raises important questions about what he calls "the fuzzy-wuzzy
psychobabblers who pass as management thinkers in our postindustrial
world."[5] According to these New Age thinkers the "information age"
has apparently spawned a new type of employee whose main motivator
is not money and who is actually offended by any suggestion that it is.
Ever the skeptic, Hargrove writes: "The fact of the matter is that we
don't like to admit that we are mainly motivated by money because it
sounds a little crass, but we all are, especially in today's ultra
materialistic world."[6]

Dr. Claire Majors, dean of library services at Minnesota State
University, agrees with Hargrove and takes his theory a step further.
In an article that appeared last year in *Library Lifelines*, Majors writes,
"Those who would argue that library employees are motivated more by
a pat on the back than by a ten dollar bill in their wallets are often simply trying to justify the wide disparity that exists between the high
salaries paid to administrators and the pitiful wages paid to working

librarians. In many respects this is a gender equity issue since the preponderance of rank and file library workers are women." She goes on to say, "Yes, participative management, positive feedback, and flexible scheduling are important, but they are effective only *after* a librarian has been paid a decent wage. First things need to come first."[7]

Picking up on Dr. Majors' point of view is librarian/activist Sherry Standish, who in an article entitled "What Do Librarians Want?" tells library directors and boards that if they are looking for nonmonetary ways to motivate their employees they should consider a bonus program with appropriate prizes. Here is her list:

WHAT MOTIVATES EMPLOYEES BESIDES MONEY

1. Bags of gold dust.
2. 14 karat gold jewelry.
3. Bottles of 1825 Dom Perignon.
4. Rembrandt originals.
5. 1957 Mickey Mantle baseball cards in mint condition.
6. Spanish pieces of eight.
7. Ownership documents to a Lexus, Infiniti, or Acura automobile.
8. Sterling silver serving sets from 18th century New England.
9. I.B.M. stock certificates.
10. Authentic artifacts from ancient Egyptian ruins.[8]

Assuming that employees are fairly paid what should a manager do to insure high staff morale?

First, let me quibble with the question's premise that high staff morale is necessarily a desirable goal. It seems to me that former Philadelphia Phillies second baseman Tod Torkelson might be a bit of an authority on this subject. After all, his book, *We May Have Finished Last But We Sure Had Fun*, is a rollicking (and sometimes bawdy) testimony to the fact that happiness does not necessarily equal productivity. According to Torkelson, the Phillies loved playing for manager Fred "Jolly" Cholly because Cholly had no rules, no curfews, and no punishments. In fact, at times he would encourage a bit of debauchery. Torkelson relates the story of the time that he was in the throes of a terrible batting slump, and Manager Cholly told him to take the night off and "get drunk and then get laid."[9] It didn't help. Not only did Torkelson's slump continue, but the Phillies ended up breaking the major league record for losses in a season.

That's not to say, of course, that unhappy employees are more productive than happy ones. The key, according to researcher Edweena Snyder is to strike a balance. She obtained the usage figures of 25 libraries and then administered a survey designed to measure the staff morale for each library. It turned out that libraries with average staff morale had significantly higher productivity figures than libraries with very high or very low morale levels.[10]

Snyder's research was so fascinating to Library Director Harold Nesbit that he decided to do a follow up study to find out what makes happy employees so unproductive. Basically, he found that there are four things that make library employees happy (besides money):

FOUR THINGS THAT MAKE LIBRARY EMPLOYEES HAPPY

1. Not working on Saturdays.
2. Not working on Sundays.
3. Not working nights.
4. Not working on holidays.

In Nesbit's words it does not take a rocket scientist to see that when you do the things that make employees happy, you in effect close the library at its busiest times and thereby insure that your productivity level will be very low.[11]

Short of administering periodical surveys what are the signs that as a manager you may be the cause of bad staff morale?

Elmer D. Jackal, professor of management studies at the Elmer S. Covington School of Librarianship, has written an article entitled "The Early Diagnosis of Organizational Distress," in which he identifies the following ten things that a manager should look for in employee behavior:

TEN SIGNS OF BAD MORALE

1. Do people have signs on their desk indicating the number of days remaining until their retirement?

2. Do a lot of the employees have a "boss pull apart doll" in their desk drawer?

3. Has someone whittled a swastika onto your office door?

4. Do you constantly have to check to see if there are tacks on the seat of your chair?

5. When you walk into a room where your employees are talking do they all of a sudden become silent?

6. Have "For Sale" signs been mysteriously springing up overnight on your front lawn?

7. When you sit down to eat lunch in the staff lounge does everyone begin talking about having to hurry downstairs to cover the reference desk?

8. Have you been getting an unusual number of flat tires?

9. When you go down to the corner tavern for happy hour after work do you regularly see your photograph mounted on the dart board?

10. Do library job ads routinely appear in your in-basket with comments like "Great career opportunity!" written all over them?[12]

Are there certain managerial styles that inherently cause bad morale?

Dr. Suzanne Findehorn's research on this subject is very instructive. She went into 14 different libraries and correlated managerial profiles with staff approval ratings. Out of that research she was able to make a list of the following nine dysfunctional management personalities:

THE NASTY NINE

1. The **Grump** gives the impression that if you do ever work up the courage to talk to him/her you will be made to feel like a "damned jackass," which is the grump's favorite expression. This person loves to complain about everything—the weather, the Cubs, the food at staff potlucks, children, spouses, even God. Sometimes you will hear rumors that beneath the grump's gruff exterior is a real teddy-bear. Don't believe it.

2. The **Wimp** can't make a decision. Consequently, policy

papers sit around for months being read and reread. Also the wimp can't stand up to anybody, not to problem employees, problem patrons, or problem administrators. And how about leadership? For the wimp that's just a concept that you read about in a library management textbook. Having a wimp for a boss is like having no boss at all.

3. The **Paranoid** is convinced that everyone is trying to get his/her job and can be found late at night after the library has closed, rifling through everyone's desk looking for evidence of a conspiracy to overthrow him/her. This person tends to be very negative toward employees who show too much ambition, enthusiasm, and intelligence. He/she likes to be surrounded with nonthreatening dullards.

4. The **Egomaniac** is fairly tolerable if you continually make reference to his/her sterling personality, superior intellect, and impeccable judgment, which is extremely difficult to do because most egomaniacs are unpleasant, unintelligent, and lacking in common sense.

5. The **Raging Bull** is heavily committed to the concept of power and tends to rule through fear and intimidation. This person's favorite expression is "I don't get ulcers; I give them."

6. The **Dweeb** rose to the management ranks simply because no one else in the organization knew anything about computers. The dweeb is usually a nice person, but he/she tends to get quite upset when people don't function as predictably as software programs.

7. The **Nitpicker** is a micromanager who knows everything about you — how much you accomplish each day, how many times your latest memo had to be rewritten to correct faulty punctuation, and how much time you spent going to the bathroom. The nitpicker is constantly observing, criticizing, and correcting. Nothing makes the nitpicker happier than finding other people's mistakes. Of all the dysfunctional managerial types, the nitpicker is the one who is most likely to be assassinated by his or her staff.

8. The **Fashion Plate** is always on the cutting edge of management trends. Last year he/she was searching for excellence, but this year the search is for the inner child. Next year look for the fashion plate to get into Zen management in a really big way.

9. The **Kennel Keeper** is the manager who loves to control people by putting them in an organizational doghouse when they disobey their master. One false move and all of a sudden you become ostracized into this supervisor's kennel of bad doggies. So you better keep smiling and wagging that tail of yours.[13]

All of these "types" sound terrible but the Kennel Keeper is really the creepiest. How do you know when you've officially entered the library's doghouse?

In his article "Notes from the Doghouse," Milford A. Smagala writes that he was sent to his library's doghouse when during a departmental staff meeting he had the temerity to question his supervisor's decision to eliminate interlibrary loans for fiction books. He writes, "it did not take long for me to know that I had been a bad dog because the very next day nobody wanted to be seen with me in the presence of my supervisor."[14] He says there are other signs that indicate that an employee has been exiled to the organizational equivalent of Siberia. What follows are some of those signs:

HOW TO KNOW THAT YOU'RE IN THE DOGHOUSE

1. Pieces of Bits and Kibbles begin appearing on the top of your desk.

2. Fellow staffers jokingly nickname you "Bowser."

3. Your desk gets moved out of the staff workroom and into the hallway to make room for a new photocopier.

4. You are not scheduled to get a Saturday off until the library remodeling project begins, and when that day arrives your supervisor even has the gall to ask you if you know how to lay carpet.

5. Your book selection responsibilities are changed from American fiction to Himalayan fiction.

6. You are told that you will be given time off to go to the annual conference of the American Library Association the next time it meets in Jersey City, New Jersey.

7. Photocopies of job ads from library trade journals begin appearing mysteriously on your desk with regularity.

8. At your yearly evaluation meeting your supervisor asks you if you've looked into the various early retirement options that your library offers even though you're only thirty-two years old.

9. You are the staff member chosen to tell Mr. Copperbottom, a convicted felon, to leave the library whenever he gets disruptive and pulls out his Swiss Army knife.

10. The only training session that your supervisor will allow you to sign up for is a seminar on how to write a résumé.[15]

Obviously the doghouse has an entrance door, but does it also have an exit? Can you ever get out once you've gotten in?

Yes, the happy ending to Milford Smagala's tale of woe is that after three years he was liberated from the doghouse when he managed to rescue his supervisor from the clutches of a would-be rapist in the parking lot after work one evening. At first this would seem to be a very lucky encounter for Mr. Smagala, but don't be fooled. He actually staged the whole thing. That's not to say that there are not more honest ways to regain the master's good graces. What follows is a list of some of Milford's other, more time consuming strategies:

HOW TO GET OUT OF THE DOGHOUSE

1. Nominate your supervisor for the Librarian of the Year award.
2. Give your supervisor expensive presents on all major holidays.
3. Offer to work your supervisor's nights and weekends.
4. Volunteer to head up the United Way drive in your department.
5. Go to your supervisor's house every six months and clean out his/her rain gutters.
6. Offer to babysit your supervisor's pets and children when he/she takes a two week cruise to the Caribbean.
7. Convert to your supervisor's religion.
8. Root for your supervisor's favorite teams.
9. Name your first born after your supervisor.
10. Marry someone on the library board.[16]

While it's easy to be critical of supervisors and managers, it's easy to forget that they are often subject to a rather significant amount of stress. What are some of the more neurotic behavioral patterns that can develop in the overstressed library manager?

Surprisingly, Pauline Laxalt, the wife of a big city public library director, seems to be the leading authority on this issue. In an article entitled "Living with and Loving a Library Director," she states categorically that the biggest problem the overstressed library director has is keeping the job at work and not bringing it home. "At the beginning of his library career when he worked reference," she writes, "my husband Arthur was a real human being when he got home. He was fun for the whole family to be with. But when he got into administration he became very bossy and businesslike. He seemed to think that we were his employees and he treated us as such. On their birthdays he gave our children performance reports for the year and on our wedding anniversary he got in the habit of issuing me a new set of goals and objectives."[17] After a great deal of family therapy the Laxalt family is back on an even keel, but in her article Pauline urges other directors to constantly be aware of their behavior at home in order to spare their families the pain that hers had to endure.

So what is the last word on library management?

1. Figure out why the library exists and what it should be doing.
2. Hire good people to do it.
3. Get out of their way.
4. Hire fewer managers than you really need.

Notes

1. Aaron Jasperson, "Measuring Reference Productivity," *Library Productivity Studies* (spring 1987) 53–67.
2. Jonathan Naismith Yardley, *Managing Libraries in Tough Times* (Strawberry Plains, TN: Farmington Press, 1991), pp. 147–151.
3. Helen Hadley Hunter, "The Library Without Offices," *New Age Librarian* (November 1989) 23.
4. *Ibid.*, 25–39.
5. Philip Hargrove, *Money Talks* (San Diego: Motivations Unlimited, 1991), p. 40.
6. *Ibid.*, p. 42.
7. Claire Majors, "Promise Her Anything But Don't Give Her Money: Thoughts on the Issue of Gender Equity and Employee Motivation," *Library Lifelines* (July 1989) 83.
8. Sherry Standish, "What Do Librarians Want?" *The Contemporary Librarian* (August 1992) 573.
9. Tod Torkelson, *We May Have Finished Last But We Sure Had Fun* (Philadelphia: Horsehide Press, 1986), p. 289.

10. Edweena Snyder, "The Morale/Productivity Matrix," *Library Productivity Studies* (winter 1988) 89–122.

11. Harold Nesbit, "The Morale/Productivity Matrix: A Follow-Up Study," *Library Productivity Studies* (fall 1991) 73–118.

12. Elmer D. Jackal, "The Early Diagnosis of Organizational Distress," *Library Management Research Quarterly* (summer 1991) 89–97.

13. Suzanne Findehorn, "Personality as a Variable in Managerial Effectiveness," *Library Management Research Quarterly* (winter 1992) 23–56.

14. Milford A. Smagala, "Notes from the Doghouse," *Today's Librarian* (August 1989) 45.

15. *Ibid.*, 46–47.

16. *Ibid.*, 49–50.

17. Pauline Laxalt, "Living with and Loving a Library Director," *Library Administrator's Update* (April 27, 1991) 13. Laxalt's warning signs of an administrator who is becoming too much of a manager at home are worth noting: (1) applies zero based budgeting to grocery shopping, (2) requires children to punch a time clock after dates, (3) begins referring to family problems as "personnel issues," (4) posts appointment hours on study door, and (5) refers to kids' weekly allowance as "wages."

BUILDINGS

Do you mean to tell me that that fat guy who sings "Day-O" all day is in charge of building my new library?

How important are buildings to libraries?

Today very few experts would dispute the commonly held view that to have a library it is very important to have a library building. While the concept of a "library without walls" brought instant notoriety to library theorist Harley A. Rockman in 1968, his vision of the library of the mind proved to have obvious limitations on cold, rainy, and dark days.[1] As a consequence, warmth, dryness, and light are conditions that are generally recognized today both by librarians and patrons as being indispensable to the furtherance of the American library movement.

Warmth, dryness, and light—are these the most important qualities that a library provides its users?

While it is the unfortunate truth that people in some parts of the world would treasure any library with a roof and a heater, many people, especially in America, expect much more from a library building than simple utilitarian minimalism. Charlotte Frances Walford put it very well in her autobiography, *Life in the Stacks,* when she wrote, "We need more than light, we need illumination; and we need more than warmth, we need love."[2] To Walford her old majestic Carnegie library was more than just a place to get in out of the rain; it was a cathedral where patrons could worship at the altar of learning. The point is that a library is much more than a mere pile of books. It is a noble idea, and the design of the building should convey this exalted sense of purpose by visually embracing the principles to which American librarianship has always been anchored—freedom and openness.

When do you know that you need a new building?

There are mathematical standards of course. William Winkleman Chesley, editor of *The Journal of Library Architecture* and author of *The Library Building: Getting from A to Z*, recommends that for every person in your service area you should have at least 1.2 square feet of building space. Therefore, according to Chesley, if your library serves a population of 50,000 people, your building should have at least 60,000 square feet.[3] Chesley is obviously counting on the fact that not all 50,000 people will show up at the library's front door at one time.

Other theorists, most notably Robin Charleson, author of *Community Based Librarianship,* argue that mathematical formulae do not provide a valid measuring stick. In Charleson's words, "quantitative standards are not really helpful since they fail to take into account the actual usage patterns of a particular service area."[4] She says that the perceptive librarian should be observant enough to recognize the actual existential signs that indicate that a community has grown out of its library. Listed below are ten examples that she gives in her book:

TEN SIGNS THAT YOUR BUILDING MAY BE TOO SMALL

1. When you leave the reference desk to get a book does a patron grab your chair and start doing homework at your desk because there is no place else to sit down and study?

2. Are you hearing rumors that some patrons are beginning to use bathroom stalls as study carrels?

3. Are you thinking seriously about relocating the cataloging department to the basement boiler room with Ralph the janitor and his pet silverfish?

4. Are your homeless patrons beginning to complain about not being able to find a place to sleep?

5. When you shelve a new book do you have to weed out an old book to make room for it?

6. Is the oldest oldest book you have left only three years old?

7. Are your resident flashers beginning to complain about having trouble finding suitable hiding places to ply their trade?

8. Are people coming to the library with folding lawn chairs?

9. Are you beginning to envision your janitor's supply closet as a potential location for your new videotape collection?

10. Do people keep asking how to get to the third floor even though your building only has two floors?

Of course it is very important to note that crowding is not the only reason why you should replace an old library building with a new one. Harold Hubbell, in his book *Maintaining Your Library Building: A Technical Manual,* emphasizes that there comes a time when buildings, like people, simply die of old age and/or disrepair. He lists the following warning signs that often occur on that road to death:

TEN SIGNS THAT YOUR BUILDING
MIGHT BE READY TO DIE

1. When it rains are you using more than seven wastebaskets to catch the water from your leaky roof?

2. In the winter is your building getting so cold that your resident flashers are starting to keep their pants on?

3. Do you routinely check out plungers to people who want to use your bathroom facilities?

4. Are students bringing flashlights to the library so they can find their way around the nonfiction stack area at night?

5. Does the American flag in the mural over the circulation desk have only 46 stars?

6. Does the building's cornerstone have the name of Andrew Carnegie on it?

7. Do the lights twinkle and dim when you turn on the photocopier?

8. Have you recently been notified by your insurance company that they will no longer offer fire coverage for your building?

9. Has the local historical society started the paperwork to have your building declared a national historical landmark?

10. Is there an old hitching post near the front door?[5]

When a library building becomes too old or too crowded doesn't the need for a new building become obvious to everyone in the community?

As librarians we would like to think so, but at times it is very difficult to convince "the powers that be" that a new library building is worth the considerable expense that it takes to design and build. In an article entitled "Political Denial," Suzanne Belihorn describes some of the reactions that she received from her political officials when she reported to them that the community had grown too large for its library:

TEN STUPID THINGS A POLITICIAN MIGHT SAY TO YOU
WHEN YOU MENTION THE NEED FOR A NEW LIBRARY

1. Why don't you move out all the tables and chairs and tell people to take the books home if they want to read them?

2. Why don't you just start a rationing program in which people with last names from A to M can only use the library on Mondays, Wednesdays, and Fridays, and people with last names from N to Z can only use the library on Tuesdays, Thursdays, and Saturdays?

3. Why don't you just build a drive-up window so that people can use the library without having to enter the building?

4. Why don't you just eliminate the fiction section? People shouldn't read books that aren't true anyway.

5. Why don't you just computerize the whole library so that people can access everything they need from home?

6. Why can't we just close the library completely and give a fifty dollar library subsidy to every family in the community to buy books with?

7. Why don't you change your operating schedule so it is open only at times that are inconvenient for public use? That would cut down on congestion.

8. Why don't you increase the check-out period from two weeks to two years? That way people won't have to come to the library as often.

9. Why don't you charge $50 for a library card? That would keep your numbers down.

10. Why don't you circulate a rumor that the library is haunted?[6]

What is the best strategy to get politicians to approve funding for new buildings?

Carol Ann Brickman, library political activist and author of the book *Your City Councilman: An Owner's Manual,* proclaims that most librarians and library trustees should shift their emphasis from "Look how a new library will help the community" to "Look how a new library will help your political career."[7]

For Brickman the key to connecting with a government official is to appeal to his or her self interest.

William A. "Buddy" Baxter, the controversial columnist for *Harper's Library Bulletin,* vehemently disagrees. He writes, "Many times local politicians are too obtuse to recognize what their best self interests are. We're not talking about rocket scientists here. After all, a good number of these people gravitated into politics because they couldn't make it in other, more respectable occupational fields."[8]

Baxter's central theory of political science is that nothing motivates a governing body like a crisis. He writes, "South Central Los Angeles goes up in flames and suddenly 50 billion dollars appear for social programs; Saddam Hussein threatens our oil supply in the Middle East and suddenly 500,000 American troops appear on his border; a tornado hits Jacknife, South Dakota, and suddenly 10 billion dollars appear for disaster relief."[9]

In his view, therefore, the best way to procure funding for a new library building is to have a crisis. "Obviously the most effective kind of crisis," writes Baxter, "is a bona fide natural disaster. The absolute best scenario is to have an earthquake, an avalanche, a flood, a tidal wave, a tornado, or a hurricane totally destroy your old library. In this case a politician is left without a choice. There are no other options but to rebuild. After all, the destruction of the old building was an act of God, and what red-blooded American politician is going to fly in the face of a divine mandate?"[10]

But Baxter is quick to point out that there is an obvious problem with bona fide natural disasters—they are hard to come by when you need them the most. That means that you will have to settle for some other, less desirable crisis. According to Baxter, "a fire is good possibility, but the problem with a fire is that it often doesn't get the job done. It is a reality that many central libraries are located near central fire stations. This fact, coupled with the vastly improved equipment that firefighters now use, almost eliminates the prospect of total destruction. This means that a fire may actually result in your worst nightmare—the old building will only be partially damaged, and your governing body will vote to have it rebuilt and remodeled. Once this happens you'll never get a new building."[11]

Obviously if your old building is bursting at the seams with books and patrons, you can't just wait around forever for an earthquake or a fire, you need to get proactive and create your own crisis. Baxter rejects such illegal strategies as arson. He says that there are three problems with arson: (a) you could get caught, (b) you might not achieve total destruction, and (c) you would be violating the ALA code of ethics.

Instead, he recommends "going the building safety route." This entails the following nine step process:

HOW TO GET A BUILDING IN NINE STEPS

1. Find out who is the fussiest, nerdiest, and most officious building safety inspector in your city's building safety department.

2. Invite this person over to your office and tell him in a very confidential way that you are afraid that your building is ready to collapse. Tell him about the cracking noises you hear at night when the second floor reading room is packed with people. Tell him about how you think the floor is beginning to sag. Tell him that you think that the book collection has grown so big and heavy that you think it's only a matter of time before the building's structural system buckles beneath it. Tell him that you are afraid hundreds of people will be killed in this death trap.

3. Then (with controlled urgency) plead with him to do a thorough inspection and evaluation of the building's structural integrity, all the while implying quite strongly that the responsibility for hundreds of lives is now solely on his back.

4. A week later when your inspector gives you his report, underline the following sentence with a bright pink highlighter: "Although there appears to be no immediate threat of collapse, the strength of the library's structural foundation has diminished over the past fifty years and this problem will need to be addressed to eliminate any possible threat to public safety in the future."

5. Send this highlighted report in a plain brown envelope (no return address) to the local paper's investigative reporter.

6. When the reporter calls you and asks about the safety of the library, refer all questions to the building inspector. After all, you're just a librarian, not a structural engineer.

7. When the story hits the paper with the headline, "LIBRARY BUILDING UNSAFE!" refer all questions from the mayor and the city manager to the building inspector. After all, you're just a librarian, not a structural engineer.

8. When hundreds of frightened citizens ("My daughter uses that library every week!") start calling your office demanding that something be done, refer them to the mayor. After all, you're just a librarian, you don't control the city's purse strings.

9. Two years later when it comes time to open your brand new library building be sure to let the mayor cut the ribbon. After all, you're just a librarian, you don't have to run for re-election.

After securing funding for a building, the next logical step is to select a library consultant. What qualifications should we look for in a building consultant?

Again, I have to take my cue from the irrepressible William A. "Buddy" Baxter. In his highly amusing, but very informative book *I Can't Install a Garbage Disposal But I Built a 20 Million Dollar Library*, he devotes an entire chapter ("Hire a Consultant Only If You're Incompetent and Have $50,000 to Waste") to debunking the conventional wisdom that the first thing a library should do before embarking upon a building project is hire an experienced library consultant. In typical Baxter hyperbole he refers to consultants as con artists, flim-flam men, thieves, pirates, swindlers, imposters, tricksters, sharks, frauds, and charlatans. Those are the nicer names. He also calls them shysters, cheats, pimps, and prostitutes.

According to Baxter most library consultants are former library directors who: (a) have taken forced retirement and are only "semilucid," (b) have taken voluntary retirement and are on cruise control, or (c) have gotten canned from their "day" jobs and are looking for an easy but lucrative career opportunity where their incompetence will not be so obvious. Baxter goes on to pose the question: "Who knows less about libraries than library directors?" and then answers it himself with the retort, "Former library directors!"[12]

To those who are put off by Baxter's heavy-handed rhetoric, I would suggest they read an article in *The Anglo-American Library Review* entitled "The Library Building Consultant: A Case Study." In this article, Sally Austin summarizes the research that she did for her master's thesis at the Broadmore School of Librarianship. Her project consisted of examining seven different building studies that consultant H. Howard Huntington completed in 1982 and 1983.[13] In a word Austin's findings were, how should I put this, rather startling. Five of the seven studies that Huntington submitted were virtually identical even though they were done for widely different libraries!

The main lesson to be learned from Austin's study is obvious: Don't bring in an arrogant, overpaid expert from the outside to tell you what your community needs and wants from a library building. That's your job! But then again if you're incompetent and have $50,000 to waste, by all means hire a consultant.

Okay, let's forget consultants. What qualification should we look for in an architect?

Again I defer to Dr. Baxter. In his chapter "Adolf Hitler Was an Architect" (in *I Can't Install a Garbage Disposal*...), he identifies the following five things that you should look for in an architect:

WHAT TO LOOK FOR IN AN ARCHITECT

(1) Honesty. Architects are like carpet salesmen. There are too many of them and they will say anything to get a job. They'd tell you they designed the Cathedral at Chartres if they thought you'd believe it. Check everything they put on their résumé and double-check everything they tell you at an interview. Designing a janitor's closet is not exactly what I call "creating" a building. Also if possible before the interview watch the parking lot and find out what kind of car they're driving. The guys who are actually going to be doing 95 percent of the work on your library design, are grunts who drive Chevys and Fords. So if an architect drives up for an interview in a Mercedes or BMW and tells you he's going to do most of the work, you know you're dealing with a liar. He's actually what is called a "principal" and all he's going to do is sit around in his office, leaf through architecture magazines, and count the money that you pay him.

(2) Humanity. One thing you must know about architects is that with them the right look is very, very important. After all, design is their job. It's the engineers who actually make a building work. Just look at the way architects dress — $1,200 Hugo Boss suits, $350 J.M. Weston dress shoes, and $70 Armani ties. But look closely at that tie. Does it have a spot on it? All you're looking for is a speck caused by a wayward piece of pasta or a dribble of French dressing. No, that's not quite it. What you're really looking for is the hint of soul or, if you prefer, a touch of humanity. Is your architect real or plastic? Look closely at that tie.

(3) Chutzpah. Architects are a lot like librarians in that the pressure to conform to a prescribed set of professional norms is very strong among them. Just look around you. The new buildings going up at any one time all sort of look the same. You know, same color, same shape, same size. Then after people get tired of that look, architects get out a different cookie cutter. What you want is a creator, not an imitator. Therefore, keep an eye out for flashes of

weirdness. Look for the architect who drives a Bug, wears a bow tie, sports an earring, has a pony tail, wears sandals, prefers purple lip gloss, munches on jujubes, wears a hat indoors, or quotes Andy Warhol.

(4) Simple Declarative Sentences. It's true that members of every profession — librarians, lawyers, shoe salesmen, and even plumbers — speak in jargon. But architects have made an art form out of their jargon and what's worse is that they use it in non–job related areas. For instance if you're ever at a cocktail party and you overhear someone talking about "positioning" a personal relationship in terms of "a series of unifying interests penetrated by shafts of individual preferences" you can almost bet that's an architect speaking about a spouse. Here's the bottom line: Architects who are incapable of using simple declarative sentences are incapable of communicating with you. The fact of the matter is architects love to "structure their conversations assymetrically" because that's an easy way for them to dominate their clients. The only way to respond to those architects, therefore, is with some jargon of your own: "Bullshit."

(5) A Feel for Literature. Your architect doesn't have to be able to quote Falstaff's speech about love from *King Henry IV*, but he or she should know that *The Catcher in the Rye* is not about baseball and that Gwendolyn Brooks is not Garth's little sister. This is a library you want your architect to design, and it should feel like a library. Ask each candidate the title of the last piece of literature that he or she read. If the answer is *Innovations in Structural Steel,* look elsewhere.[14]

What is the role of the library director in the library building project?

No one has written better on this subject than Geraldine Ruggles, director of the Smitherton Memorial Library. Her book, *I Built a Library Building and Now I'm in Analysis,* in addition to being an amusing diary of her madcap experiences as a librarian turned construction manager, is also (if you can stop laughing) very useful as a "how-to-do-it" manual. "Above all," writes Ruggles, "the library director–construction manager functions as a kind of circus clown who tries to juggle about fifteen flaming chain saws while walking on a tight rope after bungee jumping from a high wire while singing the National Anthem and saluting the American flag."[15]

Much has been written about library directors suffering from something called "Post Building Depression Symdrome." What exactly is this disorder?

Doctor-Doctor H.P. Strathmirer (he calls himself "Doctor-Doctor" because he has a doctorate in both library science and abnormal psychology, which some people think is the same thing) deals with this subject in his excellent article "Roller Coaster of the Mind: Directing the Library Building Project." According to Doctor-Doctor, the much ballyhooed "post building depression syndrome" is actually just the final valley in the roller coaster ride that all library directors take when they manage a building project. He claims it is caused by the trauma of having the great "unwashed" public actually use the brand new building. After working so hard to make everything perfect the director is now faced with the reality of muddied carpeting and soiled furniture. It can be very depressing.[16]

What are your final words of wisdom on building a library building?

In conclusion I defer to, who else, Buddy Baxter. In the chapter entitled, "Don't Name Your Building After an Ax Murderer," he offers the following three tips on the Dedication Ceremony:

1. Be sure and turn the sprinklers off, especially if your ceremony is scheduled for the library's front lawn.
2. Make sure the names of your board members are spelled correctly on the dedication plaque.
3. Don't name your building after a living person. He or she might turn out to be an ax murderer.[17]

Notes

1. Harley A. Rockman, *A Library of the Mind* (Portland: Harbor Lights Publications, 1968), p. 57.
2. Charlotte Frances Walford, *Life in the Stacks* (Emporia: Eye Shade Press, 1975), p. 193.
3. William Winkleman Chesley, *The Library Building: Getting from A to Z* (Houston: Bibliotechnical Publications, 1982), p. 134.

4. Robin Charleson, *Community Based Librarianship* (St. Louis: Booktop Press, 1988), p. 339. For a comprehensive and up to date account of the input standards and output measures controversy read Reginald Woolley's recent book *Input, Output, and Thruput: Their Strengths, Their Weaknesses, and Their Uses* (St. Cloud: Cardinal Press, 1992).

5. Harold Hubbell, *Maintaining Your Library Building: A Technical Manual* (Detroit: Greenfield Press, 1986), p. 237.

6. Suzanne Belihorn, "Political Denial," *The Contemporary Librarian* (March 1987) 19–21.

7. Carol Ann Brickman, *Your City Councilman: An Owner's Manual* (Buffalo: Public Administration Press, 1988), p. 426.

8. William Arthur Baxter, "Publically Speaking," *Harper's Library Bulletin* (January 1989) 97.

9. *Ibid.*, 98.

10. *Ibid.*, 99.

11. *Ibid.*, 100.

12. William Arthur Baxter, *I Can't Install a Garbage Disposal But I Built a 20 Million Dollar Library* (Brooklyn: H.W. Harper's Co., 1990), p. 277.

13. Sally Austin, "The Library Building Consultant: A Case Study," *The Anglo-American Library Review* (October 1991) 47–63.

14. Baxter, *I Can't Install a Garbage Disposal,* pp. 159–183.

15. Geraldine Ruggles, *I Built a Library Building and Now I'm in Analysis* (Boston: Wittleson and Franklin, 1989), p. 57.

16. H.P. Strathmirer, "Roller Coaster of the Mind: Directing the Library Building Project," *Library Lifelines* (February 1989) 62.

17. Baxter, *I Can't Install a Garbage Disposal,* pp. 201–202.

PATRONS

I need a recording of live dinosaur sounds.

Are patrons really necessary in a library?

This, of course, is a tricky question, one that conjures up that old philosophical conundrum about a tree falling in the forest. If no one is there to hear the tree fall, does it in fact make a noise? Furthermore, one might ask does the tree really fall or more to the point does the tree even exist, to say nothing of the forest?

There is, of course, a theory out and about in modern technological circles that God created men and women to give reality to His/Her universe. Think about it. What would be the point of the majestic beauties of the natural world if we were not there to experience, admire, and enjoy them. That, I firmly believe, is our cosmic purpose — to act as witness to the creation and validate God's handiwork.

A library, of course, is no different. One is tempted to say that without users a library is actually quite illogical, but that is not the case. It goes beyond illogic to nonexistence. An unused collection of books is simply that — an unused collection of books. It is not a library. Books do not become real until people read them.

Is the reverse also true, that people do not become real until they use a library?

Obviously it all depends upon how you define "real." An economist, when using the term "real wages," is not referring to the monetary value of the wages but to the true worth of the wages in terms of what they will actually buy in the marketplace of goods and services. Extrapolating, we would have to concur that realness in a person refers to the person's true worth, not the inherent value emanating from the quality of personhood. Seen in that light, it becomes obvious that although the library doesn't absolutely establish a person's realness, it does enhance it rather immeasurably. In short, patrons need libraries almost as much as libraries need patrons.

Beyond enhancing realness what are the specific reasons patrons need libraries?

For specificity, it's convenient to turn to a little article entitled "People Ask the Darnedest Things." It's written by Shirley Coppersmith, reference librarian for the Centerbury Public Library. While Coppersmith explains that reference service is often fairly routine (I need the consumer advice periodicals, I need ten sources on a term paper, I need the medical dictionaries, I need the criss-cross directory, I need the insect identification books, I need the plumbing repair section, etc.) the fact remains that patrons still articulate some rather unpredictable informational needs. For instance, Coppersmith lists twenty-five unusual requests that she fielded at the reference desk in her library in the course of only one week:

TWENTY-FIVE UNCONVENTIONAL PATRON REQUESTS

1. A cassette tape of actual dinosaur sounds.
2. A videotape of Lincoln giving the Gettysburg address.
3. The phone number for "911."
4. An explanation of how the world will end.
5. The meaning of life.
6. An explanation of where urban squirrels go to die.
7. The location of recent Tinkerbelle sightings.
8. A way to lose twenty pounds in two days.
9. How to say "Good Morning" in sign language over the phone.
10. The zip code for Mayberry, where Andy Griffith used to be sheriff.
11. Where to send a donation of twenty dollars to help pay off the four trillion dollar national debt.
12. The Blue Book price on an '89 Corsica Hatchback that is missing the hatch.
13. The best English translation of *Hamlet*.
14. How to be admitted into the Federal Witness Protection Program.
15. The name of the author of *The Diary of Anne Frank*.
16. The location of a tall yellow book with a picture of a tractor on the cover.
17. The age of a person when he or she is born.
18. Annual reports from I.B.M., General Motors, and Willy's Worms.
19. The name of the person who invented the time machine.
20. The exact location of Cicely, Alaska, where the television show "Northern Exposure" is located.
21. New novels with a lot of "good sex and violence" in them.

22. The name and number of the man who sells marijuana at the library.

23. The proper ceremony to follow for a dog's funeral.

24. The book that tells you how to find out who you were in past lives.

25. A photograph of Christopher Columbus.[1]

Do unconventional requests generally emanate from unconventional patrons?

No, not at all. This is the scary part. According to Coppersmith some of the most unusual questions come from the most normal people. It is, in her opinion, a symptom of our times that the fine line separating fiction, fantasy, and reality is becoming quite blurred. People have lost sense of the concept of actual physical existence. What they see on television and in the movies and what they read in supermarket tabloids has unfortunately become their existential frame of reference. Just remember the difficulty that former Vice President Dan Quayle had in understanding that Murphy Brown and her fatherless child were not real people. Homer Simpson is a lot more immediate to most people than their own next door neighbors.

Is the chronic overdue borrower the most troublesome type of patron?

Absolutely, but librarians have made the delinquent borrower a problem. In fact, in his book, *Fine Fetishism and the American Library Tradition*, William Pollard Jenkins traces the root of the library profession's image problem to the term "overdue fine." To support this claim, Jenkins cites research data drawn from a word association game that he played with 4,000 randomly chosen subjects. When Jenkins said the word "library," 2,944 of the 4,000 people said either "fine" or "overdue" in response. "In essence," writes Jenkins, "this means that almost 75 percent of the adult American population has a negative impression of libraries and librarians. Clearly the issue of fines is a professional Vietnam that librarians have been mired in for almost a century."[2]

In reviewing the book, Dr. Sarah Bridle Baumgarten criticizes Jenkins for attacking the traditional fine structure without giving any constructive alternatives. She writes, "Simply deploring the pettiness of the five cent fine for three hundred pages does nothing to alter the unfortunate fact that library patrons seem to need motivation in getting books back on time."[3]

The whole fines and overdue issue is probably best analyzed by Harold A. Bardley in his article "Library Justice: A Re-examination of the Delinquent Borrower." In this article Bardley claims that the punishment for any crime has two purposes — to chastise the person who committed the crime and to deter others from committing the same crime. The key, he says, is to settle upon a punishment that is not too severe for the crime, but is severe enough to discourage future transgressions. "Obviously," he writes, "if we really wanted to end delinquent borrowing once and for all we would institute the death sentence, but this would be socially unacceptable in its severity."[4] So instead we levy nickel and dime fines, which according to Bardley constitute neither a just punishment nor an effective deterrent. "In today's affluent world," writes Bardley, "the library fine has become an annoyance rather than a meaningful form of penance. In fact, some people seem to derive a twisted sense of nobility out of paying fines as though they are making a charitable donation to a worthy cause."[5]

That is precisely why, according to Bardley, that the recent trend among librarians to accept canned goods for the homeless in lieu of monetary fines is so misguided. "People who engage in delinquent borrowing should not be made to feel as though they are helping to stop world hunger. Plus everyone loves to get rid of their canned goods. Think about it. No one really enjoys eating canned peas or sweet potatoes, they'd rather give it all to the poor along with their outdated floral ties and polyester pants from the seventies. Let's not therefore *encourage* people to become delinquent borrowers."[6]

Instead, Bardley challenges librarians to develop punishments that will fit the crime. Drawing on his experience as a wayward parochial school student, he writes, "Contrary to general perception, the pre–Vatican Council Roman Catholic schools of the 1950s were highly disciplined institutions, not because of the much publicized use of corporal punishment but because of the judicious use of the punitive essay. In encouraging good behavior, the threat of being hit across the knuckles with a ruler is not nearly as effective as the threat of being forced to write a 5,000 word essay comparing the Old and New Testaments on the issue of crime and punishment. While the bruise from the ruler can be worn as a badge of honor, the scars from submitting to the torture of writing a long essay are both invisible and unhealing."[7]

This is a point that librarians should not take lightly. The nickel fine—the financial equivalent of being rapped lightly on the knuckles—has been a complete failure in changing the behavior of library patrons. People are as delinquent now as they were in the days before the nickel fine. This assertion is confirmed by the historical research of Dr. Pamela A. Perkins, professor of the history of American librarianship at the Sterling Institute of Information Studies. Perkins has compared circulation records before the use of fines, which became widespread at the same time that masses of immigrants from Eastern Europe and Asia began to crowd our cities (was the fine concept instituted to discourage the poor from using public libraries?), and after, and has found no significant change in patron punctuality.[8]

This all means, according to Bardley, that it's time for a change. "Look at the cultural landscape," he proclaims, "and you will find that the American people are functionally and culturally illiterate. They need a public library that demands a modicum of standards. Here's where the overdue dilemma can be turned into a positive. Next time a patron brings in a book that is two or more weeks overdue, the penalty should not be in the pocketbook but in the mind. Make the patron write a 1,500 word essay critiquing the book(s) overdue. No critique, no more borrowing privileges. Force people to exercise their mind; coerce them to pick up pen and write. Is the American library an outpost of literacy or not?"[9]

Have there been any other innovations in the area of overdue punishments?

Actually there have been. Bardley's ideas have stimulated a lot of new thinking in this area. Bernadine Bauer, head of circulation for the Pepperwood (Tennessee) Public Library, in an article that she wrote for *Support Staff Quarterly* entitled "Make the Punishment Fit the Crime," says that the overdue punishment should be tailored to the length of time that the book is overdue and it should also correlate with what the book is about. If, for instance, someone returned a fitness book two weeks overdue, that person should be required to run two laps around the outside of the library. If the book in question were a diet book, the offender should be made to lose two pounds.[10] I'm not sure, however, what Ms. Bauer would require in the case of an overdue sex manual, but it's fun to imagine the possibilities.

In conclusion this type of advanced thinking is certainly preferable to the ideas that seem to have been generated in the middle of the 1980s when a number of circulation personnel were suggesting that only by deploying a more draconian penal policy (breaking fingers and putting people in public stocks) would libraries be able to stem the obvious decline in patron morals.

Why are librarians so obsessed with delinquent borrowers?

The main reason, according to Dr. Wolfgang Lipkind, consulting behavioral psychologist for the Blackstone Institute of Library Studies, is that librarians as a group are very honest. In fact, his research indicates that next to Roman Catholic nuns, librarians are the most honest professional group in America. Librarians, because they are so truthful, find it exceedingly difficult to tolerate patron lies. On the other hand, chronically delinquent borrowers are one of the most dishonest study cohorts that Dr. Lipkind has ever researched. The clash between the two groups is, therefore, almost inevitable.[11]

Dr. Lipkind's scholarly research is nicely complemented by the "real world" writings of Wilma W. Wilson, the self proclaimed "circ clerk in tennis shoes." In an article entitled "Overdues, Lies, and Library Patrons" she gives the following list of lies that she has been told at the circulation desk of her library:

LIES THAT OVERDUE BORROWERS TELL

1. I had a visitation from an angel and he told me that this book was demonic and that I should keep it checked out indefinitely so that no one could read it and be corrupted by it.

2. My wife is on the verge of a nervous breakdown and this book was the only thing that was keeping her sane.

3. On my way home from the library I was abducted by aliens. They didn't return me (and my library book) to earth for three months.

4. I took my book on vacation two months ago. Unfortunately

the airlines lost my luggage and the book was in the luggage. They just found it yesterday.

5. I thought that the President should read this book so I sent it to him. He didn't return it until last week. He wrote that he was sorry that the book was late but that he needed it to help him with his economic policy.

6. I am toilet training my two year old son, and he refuses to get on the toilet unless I read him this book.

7. My house is haunted and this book is the only thing I've found that is effective in warding off evil spirits.

8. When I checked this book out some crazy college student followed me out of the library, pointed a gun at me, and grabbed the book from me. He said he needed it desperately for a class and that he would return it when he was finished with it. I didn't get it back for six months.

9. I went into the hospital for a gall bladder operation and took the book with me for something to read during my stay. My roommate, a terminal cancer patient, took a fancy to the book and so I let him read. He liked the book so much that I didn't have the heart to ask for it back when my stay in the hospital was over. He died last week and the book was finally returned to me by his brother.

10. I kept this book out so long because I knew that I am the only person in the community smart enough to understand it.[12]

Enough about delinquent borrowers. How about the homeless person? Isn't the homeless person a much more troublesome problem?

Absolutely not. "Give me a homeless person any day over the shrill yuppie mommie who expects you to motivate her L.L. Bean clad five year old son to read and understand Sartre's *Being and Nothingness*." These words can only belong to the irrepressible Buddy Baxter, that gadfly of library literature who actually claims to have been homeless for the better part of his postgraduate education.

"There I was," writes Baxter in his semiautobiographical manifesto, *Insincere Regrets*, "at the D.U. Graduate Library School with about 73¢ in my pocket, which I couldn't waste on anything as mundane as rent. So I went homeless the whole time that I was working on my M.L.S. Where did I sleep? Well, I may have been homeless but I always had a home and I never crashed with friends, not because

I didn't want to impose but because I didn't have any friends. Actually I didn't have to look much further than that grand old lady Mary Reed for shelter. Mary Reed was the name for the D.U. library. They have since built a shiny new library and turned Mary Reed into an office building of sorts. Actually I think they got it backwards because the new library with its mirrored walls and expansive hallways has all the character of an insurance company headquarters, and Mary Reed with its Gothic spires and ivy covered walls reeks of the well worn refinement that one hopes to find in a library on a tree lined college campus.

"Not only was Mary Reed a dignified old lady, but she was wonderfully complex, full of secret passageways, nooks, and crannies. It was not challenging to find guest quarters there. In fact I found first rate accommodations for three straight months in an old subterranean storage room that the college had designated as its official bomb shelter. Remember that my sojourn at D.U. was during the Nixon seventies, a felicitous period of détente with Russia when our sense of civil defense was on the decline. We were more concerned with the reality of what was actually happening in Vietnam than with the theoretical spectre of nuclear war with the Soviets, and so this room, this neglected relic of the Cuban Missile Crisis, became my private quarters. It was nothing if not convenient, stocked as it was with cots and potable water and even canned snacks. I slept and ate well and bothered no one.

"Eventually, of course, I was discovered. Fortunately my discoverer was understanding. He too was homeless, and we agreed that the resources of our facility could accommodate two people as easily as one, and although my new roommate was a bit of a snorer we managed to coexist quite nicely. From him — let's call him Jack — I learned that the homeless, the hardcore homeless, far from being intentionally troublesome, value elusiveness above all else. They don't want to be noticed because to be noticed is to eventually be harassed by both do-gooders and do-baders. Most homeless simply want to be left alone.

"My acquaintance with Jack was probably the most valuable learning experience I had during library school because it gave me a realistic frame of reference from which to deal with what library editorialists in the 1980s would sanctimoniously call 'Our Homeless Problem.' To me, of course, the homeless have never been a problem."[13]

In fact, Baxter went on to do more writing and reflecting upon the homeless and their use of the library, and in an article entitled "A

Homeless Manifesto" he puts forth the following ten advantages of having homeless people use your library:

TEN ADVANTAGES OF HOMELESS PATRONS

1. They never ask "Where is the rest room?" because they have a sixth sense for that sort of thing.
2. They never come in ten minutes before closing and ask for ten magazine articles on capital punishment for a term paper that is due tomorrow.
3. They never threaten to call the mayor and complain about services.
4. They are never in a hurry.
5. They never put suggestions in the suggestion box.
6. They never have overdues (mainly because they never check out books).
7. They never bring unruly children into the library with them.
8. They never steal the stock market listings out of the *Wall Street Journal.*
9. They never clip coupons out of *Ladies Home Journal.*
10. They never smell as bad as some of the fragrance cards that are often affixed to new magazines.[14]

But isn't it true that the homeless do engage in harassing activities such as flashing, mooning, and stealing women's shoes?

To say that the homeless never engage in these activities would obviously be tilting against statistical probabilities, but the fact is that recent research reveals that the homeless don't engage in these activities to any greater degree than the nonhomeless. In an article entitled "Flashers, Foot Fetishists, Mooners, Moonies, Perverts, Professors, and Republicans," Professor Harold Sterling-Higginbottom reports on research that he did in seven urban public libraries and five urban academic libraries. What Sterling-Higginbottom attempted to do was examine the police records for each library with regard to patrons who had been arrested for "crimes and misdemeanors of harassment." What he found out was that less than 6 percent (5.7 to be exact) of these offenses were committed by homeless individuals. "Harassment," claims Dr. Sterling-Higginbottom, "is not limited to any one socioeconomic group. The wealthiest Republican is as likely to engage in harassment as the poorest homeless person."[15]

Which types of patrons are the most troublesome for library staffers?

In an article entitled "A Rogues Gallery: Patrons Who Drive Librarians Nuts," Erma Denkinger identifies her "ten most wanted problem patrons":

THE TEN MOST WANTED PROBLEM PATRONS

1. The Magazine Hog. This person takes possession of up to ten current magazines at a time and then retreats to a nook or cranny in the library in the library where he cannot be easily found. This wouldn't be too bad if the magazines in question were things like *Ceramics Monthly* or *Microbiology Today,* but the magazine hog always lays claim to fun stuff like *People, Cosmo,* and *Rolling Stone.* This is definitely a problem for patrons who do not want to have to read *Ceramics Monthly* while waiting for the magazine hog to finish with *Cosmo.* Invariably the reference librarian is called in to referee, and invariably the hog says something like, "Has the Library Board passed a rule that says I cannot take ten magazines at once?"

2. The Coupon Clipper. Where does it say in the Library Bill of Rights that patrons have a First Amendment right to clip coupons out of magazines and newspapers? There is nothing more maddening than to be reading an absorbing article about the marital problems of the Royal Family and come to a gap in the page where a coupon for Glad sandwich bags has been clipped.

3. The CD-ROM Printer Junkie. We should have seen this coming when we installed computers and printers in our libraries for public use. Let people print for free and they'll print to their hearts' delight — not because they need the information but because there is something hypnotic about watching a printer print endlessly and tirelessly. It's almost like watching a player piano in action. Some television commercials on knowing when to say when might be really helpful here.

4. The Sleeper. Don't misunderstand this one. Sleeping in a library is fine. All the latest research shows a direct link between sleep and mental acuity. Since we obviously need sleep to think clearly, it is not difficult at all to accept sleeping as a valid library activity. Sometimes, however, sleepers become irresponsible, specifically when they fall asleep (face down) on magazines and newspapers that other patrons want to read. From a librarian's standpoint, this presents a very ticklish situation. Do you wake the patron up and risk the wrath of a person who has been abruptly returned from dreamland or do you try to extricate the newspaper ever so gently out from under the patron's nose?

5. People with Self-Contradicting Requests. Reference librarians are steeled to finesse their way through impossible requests: where can I buy an H.O. scale model of the White House; how can I get grape Kool Aid stains out of a white carpet; and is there a method by which I can really toilet train my one-year-old in twenty-four hours? People don't really expect you to find anything helpful in these areas; they simply hope that they'll get lucky. That is not the case, however, when someone asks for a nice, clean wholesome contemporary novel with no sex, violence, or coarse language. Good luck meeting expectations on that one. Or how about the patron who wants an easy explanation of the meaning of "quantum physics." There ought to be one, but there isn't. It's a hopelessly complex subject. You feel very stupid.

6. Ten Minutes to Closing; Ten Sources to Go. It's 8:50 on a Monday evening—ten minutes to closing and your feet hurt, your stomach is growling, your head aches. It's Miller time—time to catch the second half of Monday night football. In anticipation you begin closing out your reference statistics, signing off your computer, and straightening up the chaos on the desk in front of you. Then this twerp marches in and asks you for ten sources for a term paper he is doing on the subject of the reproductive cycle of the fruit fly in tropical climates.

7. I Know the Mysteries of the Universe and of Your Next Door Neighbor. You're a nice person. You master the little things that separate good service from exceptional service. You get to know your patrons by name. You wish them a good morning and implore them to have a good day. Some of them think you mean it. So while you're trying to do some work they talk and they talk and they talk—about the big bang theory, the failure of representative democracy, and some of the weird stuff that your next door neighbors have been hanging on their clotheslines while you've been at work staffing the reference desk. Only the latter is of the least bit of interest to you.

8. You're a Public Servant and You Have to Eat Garbage and Like It. Isn't it time that we retire the phrase "public servant" from our conversational vernacular? Wasn't the Emancipation Proclamation signed in 1863? Apparently some people don't seem to have noticed. These are the people who when you hesitate to read them 78 different stock quotations over the phone remind you that you are their tax supported slave.

9. You're Just a Typical Bureaucrat. It's hard, in this day and age to think of a more stinging insult than to call someone a "typical bureaucrat." We'd rather be called a mass murderer because at least mass murderers get some sympathy ("He was so misunderstood. His father beat him, his mother abused him, and his teachers never gave him a chance.") But bureaucrats get nothing but ridicule (can't get a job in the private sector), calumny (doesn't do anything all day but drink coffee and read books), and blame (the reason we have a four trillion dollar deficit is because we have too many bureaucrats). It's the hardest thing in the world, therefore, at the end of a long, stressful day not to strangle the patron who calls you a "typical bureaucrat" when you refuse to keep the library open an extra hour so that he can finish the work he is doing in the microfilm room.

10. Back Home Our Library Had "The Texas Chain Saw Massacre" on Videotape. The most effective way to insult a library is not to say, "This library stinks," but rather to say, "This library makes the one in my hometown look like the Library of Congress." No doubt about it, librarians are real sensitive about having their libraries compared unfavorably with other libraries, especially when the comparison is made on rather dubious grounds like who's got the best collection of disgusting horror movies. But some patrons just love to rub it in when we are unable to meet their rather plebeian tastes. It's maddening to be insulted by a cultural cretin.[16]

What can librarians do when they are verbally abused by patrons?

Unfortunately, not much. Librarians in many respects have to be customer services experts who are skilled at defusing angry patrons and are level headed enough not to become unglued by insults even though the temptation may be great to hurl back an insult or two at the offending patron. Alphonse Hood, head of reference services for the Footbridge Public Library, has compiled a list of insults that librarians can use during their very last week before retirement, the one time when they are immune from reprimands or discipline:

ELEVEN HANDY INSULTS FOR LIBRARIANS
WHO WANT TO TAKE A PARTING SHOT
AT VERBALLY ABUSIVE PATRONS

1. PATRON: "Do what I say! I'm a taxpayer and I pay your salary."
LIBRARIAN: "Here's your dime back. Now leave me alone."

2. PATRON: "This book is inappropriate, it could be harmful to the community, and it should be taken off the shelf!"
LIBRARIAN: "What, do you think the book is going to jump up and bite someone as soon as he walks into the library?"

3. PATRON: "I don't think this fine is fair. I'm not going to pay it."
LIBRARIAN: "Have it your way, we'll just send Vito and Rocco out to your house to collect it."

4. PATRON: "Look, I don't care if you are helping other people, I'm in a hurry. Show me where the do-it-yourself books are, right now!"
LIBRARIAN: "Oh, go do it yourself."

5. PATRON: "I don't care if the library does close in five minutes. I need fifteen sources on the subject of suicide!"
LIBRARIAN: "Here's Dr. Kevorkian's new how-to book. Follow the instructions very carefully and you won't need the other fourteen sources."

6. PATRON: "I'm very upset! Your computer says that the book I need is "Available," but I can't find it on the shelves!"
LIBRARIAN: "So go scream at the computer."

7. PATRON: "It's absolutely ridiculous that you won't let me check out *The Thomas Register* just because it's a reference book! I'm going to call the mayor!"
LIBRARIAN: "Look, Buddy, the city's going broke, the North Side Bridge just got washed away by the flood, riots are breaking out in Center City, the roof over the mayor's head has a leak, and yesterday his son ran over a lawyer's kid. So make my day, call the mayor."

8. PATRON: "It's about time you finally got this mystery for me! I've only been on the waiting list for five months! You have to be the most inefficient librarian in the world!"

LIBRARIAN: "I sincerely hope you enjoy the mystery. It has a surprise ending. The priest turns out to be the murderer."

9. PATRON: "What do you mean my two year old can't attend the five year old story hour! She's gifted!"

LIBRARIAN: "If she's so gifted why is she still in diapers?"

10. PATRON: "I can't believe how bad this library is! I hate your hours, I hate your collection, and I hate the people who work here, and that includes you!"

LIBRARIAN: "If you don't shut up, I'll lock you up in the tech services workroom with our catalogers for a day."

11. PATRON: "Why don't you have Madonna's new book? Are you a censor?"

LIBRARIAN: "Why do you want Madonna's new book? Are you a pervert?"[17]

While dealing with the verbally abusive patron can be a real strain, requiring tact and forbearance, how should a librarian deal with a physically or sexually harassing patron?

Bingo! Now we've hit the real problem patron. The biggest myth about library work is that it is safe, secure, and quiet. Maybe there's a sense of safety for people working away from the public in isolated offices, but for the public services librarian, there is always the risk factor to contend with, and in many cases public services librarians and their support personnel go about their jobs with an underlying feeling of fear. In an article entitled "The Library Jungle," Rosemary Atherton characterizes the library workplace today as an increasingly hostile environment. "More and more," she writes, "patrons manifest their complaints about service with more than mere verbal abuse. Now they threaten physical harm either to the librarian personally or to her car, house, or even family members. The practice of civility in this country is eroding quickly."[18]

Even more common than the threat of physical violence, however, is the reality of sexual harassment. The results of the survey I ran in the *Wilson Library Bulletin* on the issue of librarians and sex revealed a shockingly high rate of harassment by library patrons: 78 percent of the women who sent back the questionnaire indicated that they had been victimized by sexual harassment by patrons. Unfortunately, this is in many ways a hidden problem because many employees are too embarrassed to report these activities and many supervisors simply don't want them reported. As a profession we have dangerously put the rights of the patron ahead of the rights of the library staff. The sad truth is that many of our most powerful professional spokespeople simply do not want something mundane like employee safety to interfere with their heroic advocacy of the patron's intellectual freedom.

Why is this the case?

In an article entitled "Are We Really in the Same Profession?" Stuart H. Cromwell makes the point that there are basically two types of people who claim to be in the library profession — those who actually work in libraries and those who do not. According to him, the first group includes such people as children's librarians, reference librarians, catalogers, and library administrators. These are the folks who keep our libraries running. They are the ones who, among other things, acquire books, input bibliographic data, serve the public, do story hours, and haggle for budgets. Cromwell calls these people "librarians."

The second group includes but is not limited to library trade journal writers and editors, library school professors, consultants, and library association employees. These are the people who do research about libraries, write about libraries, talk about libraries, theorize about libraries, plan for libraries, but do not actually work in libraries. Cromwell calls them "library scientists."

He points out that the irony of our profession is that the overwhelming number of people in the profession belong in the first sector and yet they exist as a kind of vast silent majority that is rarely heard from and rarely listened to. The library scientists, on the other hand, are the movers and shakers of the profession. The irony, of course, is that the library scientists are remote from the patron. As a result, librarians often look at the work of the library scientists and ask themselves, "Are we really in the same profession?"

For instance, recently a large conference was held in which a number of national "library leaders" got together to discuss the future of the public library. Cromwell points out that he knew that most of these "leaders" were library scientists because the future that they were talking about was the year 2100. According to Cromwell, "Library scientists like to talk in terms of centuries. To librarians, however, the future is five minutes from now."[19]

The huge chasm that exists between library scientists and librarians explains why verbal, physical, and sexual harassment by library patrons is ignored. The library scientists are not aware of the problem nor do they want to be. They would rather sit comfortably in their ivory towers and pontificate pompously about the importance of intellectual freedom in a democratic society. The result is that harassment by patrons is not a big issue in the profession, and when it does become a big issue (as in the famous Morristown case) the library scientists champion the patron's right to access rather than the librarian's right to safety.

Notes

1. Shirley Coppersmith, "People Ask the Darnedest Things," *The Irrepressible Librarian* (December 1989) 39.

2. William Pollard Jenkins, *Fine Fetishism and the American Library Tradition* (Knoxville: McDougall and Sons, Publishers, 1982), p. 149.

3. Sarah Bridle Baumgarten, "*Fine Fetishism and the American Library Tradition:* A Review," *Harper's Library Bulletin* (spring 1983) 69.

4. Harold A. Bardley, "Library Justice: A Re-examination of the Delinquent Borrower," *Journal of Library Philosophy* (summer 1985) 85.

5. *Ibid.*, 89.

6. *Ibid.*, 93.

7. *Ibid.*, 95.

8. Pamela A. Perkins, "Patron Punctuality: An Historical Review of the Effectiveness of the Library Fine," *Journal of American Library History* (winter 1987) 452.

9. Bardley, "Library Justice: A Re-examination of the Delinquent Borrower," 94.

10. Bernadine Bauer, "Make the Punishment Fit the Crime," *Support Staff Quarterly* (fall 1988) 307.

11. Wolfgang Lipkind, "Values Clash: A Comparative Study of the Integrity Quotients of Librarians and Delinquent Borrowers," *Journal of Library Ethics* (spring 1989) 52–63.

12. Wilma Wilda Wilson, "Overdues, Lies, and Library Patrons," *Support Staff Quarterly* (winter 1990) 451.

13. William Arthur Baxter, *Insincere Regrets* (Brooklyn: H.W. Harper's Co., 1990), pp. 217–219.

14. William Arthur Baxter, "A Homeless Manifesto," *Harper's Library Bulletin* (January 1992) 57.

15. Harold Sterling-Higginbottom, "Flashers, Foot Fetishists, Mooners, Moonies, Perverts, Professors, and Republicans," *Journal of Library Ethics* (spring 1992) 134.

16. Erma Denkinger, "A Rogues Gallery: Patrons Who Drive Librarians Nuts," *The Irrepressible Librarian* (November 1991) 53.

17. Alphonse Hood, "So's Your Mother: Handy Insults for Lame Duck Librarians," *The Irrepressible Librarian* (March 1992) 19.

18. Rosemary Atherton, "The Library Jungle," *Harper's Library Bulletin* (April 1992) 87.

19. Stuart H. Cromwell, "Are We Really in the Same Profession?" *The Contemporary Librarian* (March 1989) 61.

ASSOCIATIONS

Sarah, I'd love to chat, but I'm off to the nonsmoking, antiwar, pro-choice, environmentally conscious, gender neutral program on culturally diverse subject headings.

Are library associations necessary?

Necessary is not the right word. Inevitable is more like it, especially in light of one of the recent findings of Gerhard Carpmeyer, the noted anthropologist, who has found evidence that suggests that as far back as 20,000 years ago stone age spear makers in France came together to form the first association organized on the basis of vocation. One of the most convincing pieces of evidence he found is a series of cave drawings depicting the following three scenes: (a) two or three men examining collections of spear heads that are exhibited neatly on the tops of large rock outcroppings, (b) thirty men sitting in a room watching another man demonstrate a spear carving technique, and (c) five or six men standing around by the fireplace at night, chatting, and drinking something out of an earthen pot. Carpmeyer says that these three drawings depict the three main elements of association conventions: exhibits, programs, and cocktail parties.[1]

What role do library associations play in the modern world?

Ostensibly to support the cause of libraries, library funding, and librarians, but the real reason according to Helena Figtower, Ph.D., is more psychologically complex. In her new book *Guilty by Association: Why Librarians Love to Join Professional Organizations*, Figtower explains that there are two main emotional reasons why librarians form and join associations — validation and empowerment. First, most librarians feel misunderstood and disrespected by the world at large, and a library association is a place where that understanding and respect is readily forthcoming. In Figtower's words, "Nobody respects a librarian more than another librarian."[2] Second, most librarians feel great frustration over the lack of control they have over their libraries due to the fact that library funding is almost always determined by non-librarians — politicians, regents, board members, and public administrators. By contrast, library organizations are totally funded, operated, and governed by librarians. "The association," she writes, "is therefore a place of empowerment for its members."[3]

The American Library Association is the largest library association in the world. What are its good points and bad points?

In an article entitled "Good Things About Bad Organizations and Bad Things About Good Organizations," Itinia Needleman points out that while the American Library Association has been around for over a hundred years, it is like any other large professional organization in that membership to it has both advantages and disadvantages. What follows is her list of these strengths and weaknesses, and you will notice that the good things outweigh the bad:

THIRTEEN GOOD THINGS ABOUT
THE AMERICAN LIBRARY ASSOCIATION

1. It keeps library directors busy and out of everybody's hair.
2. It provides full-time jobs for over 150 people, many of whom are librarians.
3. It provides a good excuse for librarians to take a vacation every summer at the taxpayer's expense.
4. It provides wonderful material for library satirists to poke fun at.
5. It gives you something to put down on your résumé under "Organizations."
6. It has never lobbied against gun control.
7. Its headquarters is not located in Cleveland.
8. It has never had Dick Nixon, Dan Quayle, or Andrew Dice Clay as its keynote speaker.
9. Its members do not wear white sheets over their heads.
10. It does not have an official song.
11. It has not yet changed its name to "The American Library and Information Science Association."
12. It put Miss Piggy on a READ poster.
13. It has never put Sylvester Stallone on a READ poster.[4]

NINE BAD THINGS ABOUT
THE AMERICAN LIBRARY ASSOCIATION

1. It never meets in Maui.
2. It sometimes meets in Dallas in July.
3. It often meets in Chicago in the middle of winter.
4. It has something called "The Committee on Committees."
5. The food served in the convention hall is always terrible and terribly overpriced.
6. It has an annual "Fun Run."

7. The word "Vision" occurs too frequently in its programs.
8. It has never had Woody Allen as a keynote speaker.
9. Its official necktie is grey, teal, and purple.[5]

But isn't it true that for all its good points the American Library Association can become more important for some librarians than their "real" library job?

This is true. While associations play an important part in promoting and developing professions they can sometimes take on an importance out of all proportion to their inherent value. Sylvia Abbott Hines has studied this situation as it relates to librarians and explains that this most often occurs when the librarian (a) sees association activities as the best way to further career goals, (b) is bored at his or her "real" job, or (c) is in a social rut and needs to meet new people. According to Hines, in most cases this is not a serious long-term problem, but if a librarian begins reading the official minutes of the ALA Council and the official proceedings of the ALA Executive Board on a regular basis this could be a sign of a need to find alternative leisure time activities.[6]

What can be done to make ALA a more effective organization?

Long time ALA member Harland Bodan Falkner (would you believe 61 years of continuous service) put down his thoughts on this matter shortly before his death (he died falling down the escalator trying to get to the main exhibit floor in San Francisco's Moscone Center) in an article entitled "I Love My Wife But She Could Make Some Improvements — The Same Goes for A.L.A." Here is what he suggested:

SEVEN WAYS TO IMPROVE A.L.A.

1. Get Dr. Ruth to write a sex advice column for the quarterly journal published by the Library Collections and Technical Services Round Table.
2. Design and market an official A.L.A. bolo tie.
3. Send boxer shorts decorated with the international library symbol to all new members.

4. Replace the annual A.L.A. Fun Run with lap swimming in the conference hotel's hot tub.

5. Hold wet tee shirt contests for librarians worried about their staid image.

6. Eliminate all A.L.A. candidate debates and replace them with mud wrestling contests.

7. Get Madonna to present seminars on "How to Do an Instant Image Makeover" for male librarians who wear pocket protectors and for female librarians who wear wool socks under their sandals.[7]

With its extensive catalog of official paraphernalia (posters, neckties, scarfs, pencils, bookmarks, tee shirts, squeeze bottles, incentive stickers, iron-on transfers, reading logs, coach caps, bookbags, bibliographies, tip sheets, time lines, murals, postcards, notecards, luggage tags, quick clips, photonovels, radio spots, t.v. commercials, frisbees, banners, pamphlets, genre lists, achievement certificates, pins, totebags, jewelry, dolls, stuffed animals, finger puppets, key tags, hand stamps, signs, program guides, and coffee mugs) is ALA getting to be overly commercialized?

Not according to Edna O. Westby, whose recent article entitled "I Joined A.L.A. to Get the Paul Newman READ Poster" appeared in the "Viewpoint" section of *Library Lifelines*. Westby, a reference librarian in an American military library in Saudi Arabia, loves the ALA READ posters because they keep her in touch with American popular culture. She is also very partial to the ALA iron-on transfers and the ALA postcards. "These official paraphernalia make me feel like an integral part of the library profession even though I am six thousand miles away from 50 E. Huron Street. In fact I would like to see A.L.A. market other official products. For instance, it can get very lonely here in the Arabian desert and I wouldn't mind spending some time with an official A.L.A. lifesize inflatable doll of a good looking cataloger or reference librarian."[8]

In the last few years ALA has come under attack for getting too political. It has, for instance, opposed the war in Iraq, boycotted the state of Arizona for failing to observe Martin Luther King's birthday as a state holiday, and criticized Israel for violating basic principles of intellectual freedom. Are these types of pronouncements appropriate for a professional organization to make?

I would have to subscribe to the comments of Herbert Whitehead Westmoreland, who in an article entitled "Hey ALA, Do You Think You Could Do Something About the Hole in the Ozone?" wrote: "The American Library Association has a constitutional right to assemble and express its opinion on any subject at all, but in pontificating on issues that have absolutely nothing to do with libraries in America it careens between pomposity and absurdity. One wonders why ALA stopped with the Iraqi War and Israeli censorship. Doesn't it care about acid rain, the extinction of the snail darter, and the depletion of the ozone layer? I'm truly disappointed that these issues are not being addressed."[9]

What can be done to make the American Library Association more relevant to the everyday lives of librarians?

While ALA is certainly a large organization with a plethora of roundtables, divisions, and sections, Michael D. Unseld has suggested yet another type of entity that ALA needs to develop in order to foster an atmosphere of real sharing and caring within this large organization. He proposes the following series of networks in an article entitled "Librarians Who Need Librarians Are the Luckiest Librarians in the World":

EIGHT NETWORKS THAT A.L.A. SHOULD SPONSOR

1. NECRONET. This is the perfect organization for librarians who want to network with deceased library practitioners. By communicating through individuals qualified in the art of the occult, this network provides contemporary librarians an opportunity to match wits with the likes of Melvil Dewey, Isadore Gilbert Mudge and Constance Winchell. This organization also gives ALA members an opportunity to keep their membership alive even after death.

2. CHOCNET. It's no secret that the library profession's drug of choice is chocolate. This network gives the true chocolate lovers in the profession an opportunity to get together and have chocolate festivals celebrating the joy that only chocolate can give. "EAT

CHOCOLATE UNTIL YOU FAINT" is a good motto for this organization. Never forget: eating chocolate to excess is legal in all fifty states.

3. NERFNET. Nerf basketball is an activity that is on the rise among administrative types. Not only is it trendy to hang a nerf hoop in your office but it is also a good way to deal with job stress. It's much better to slam-dunk a nerf ball than one of your employees. The purpose of NERFNET is to organize a single-elimination Nerfball tournament at every ALA Midwinter Meeting (which always meets right in the middle of the Nerfball season). It's a surefire way to increase midwinter attendance. A lot of people who have no interest in going to Chicago in January might do it if they knew they could become the Nerfball champion of ALA.

4. HAIRNET. This is a support group that is set up to deal with the librarian/hair issue. Many librarians are very concerned about the "hair-in-a-bun" stereotype, but they need support and encouragement to try something different. That is the purpose of this group, to provide that care, that sympathy, and that support. Changing hairstyles is one of the most traumatic things that a person can do because when you change your hairstyle you change your persona.

5. FISHNET. This is an organizational option for those librarians who are passionate about fishing and who are tired of the whole hospitality suite, cocktail party, and wine and cheese reception rat race. These librarians don't want to go to boring convention social events, they want to fish during their conference leisure time, which can sometimes be very challenging. For instance, where do you fish in Dallas in the middle of July? It's the job of FISHNET to find out.

6. DRAGNET. Cross-dressing is the decided preference of millions of Americans, some of whom are librarians. Since cross-dressing is not completely socially acceptable in our country, those who engage in this practice need support and understanding. That's the purpose of DRAGNET, to put cross-dressers in touch with each other once a year at conference time.

7. HORNET. The closets of America are filled with unused trumpets, French horns, trombones, and tubas. Isn't it a shame that people who slaved over these instruments in high school rarely get a chance to play them after graduation? The purpose of HORNET is to give horn playing librarians an opportunity to get together during annual conferences and make some noise.

8. BITCHNET. Since librarians do very stressful work under

some very stressful conditions, they need a chance periodically to let their emotions all hang out so as not to get so pent up with frustration that they run the risk of chewing out a colleague or patron. The purpose of bitchnet is to put a bunch of overstressed librarians in a room, close the door, and let them scream at each other until they get it all out of their system. It's very therapeutic.[10]

Why does the American Library Association have "conferences" rather than "conventions"?

Let's take a page out of the book *Bibliospeak* by Frank Slocum. He writes: "Librarians have conferences and not conventions for the same reason that people of refinement eat pasta, not spaghetti. It's a matter of image. Most librarians are tax supported institutions and as a rule most taxpayers do not get a thrill out of sending public employees on out-of-state trips unless, of course, a plausible argument can be made that the out-of-state trip is a legitimate continuing education opportunity that will enhance the employee's knowledge base and will result in increased on the job productivity. That's why librarians have conferences. 'Conference' is a serious sounding word that connotes serious things: lectures, speeches, programs, seminars, workshops, classes, formal papers, and panel discussions. 'Convention,' on the other hand, is a rowdy word that connotes rowdy things: balloons, noisemakers, firecrackers, dart boards, beer kegs, parties, hot tubs, and rooftop volleyball games. Plumbers have 'conventions.' Librarians have conferences."[11]

What is the real benefit of going to library conferences?

Ostensibly, librarians go to conferences to listen to boring lectures, to walk through boring exhibits, and to attend boring meetings. But everyone knows that the real reason librarians go to conferences is to commingle with other librarians for a variety of reasons — to talk shop, to gossip, and to look for jobs. It's always a very nice experience to hobnob with people who understand you. For instance, Edward W.S. Weintraub gets his biggest kick from hanging around cataloger parties and catching snippets of cataloger conversations. He claims that it's much more fun than sitting in on a lecture on *AACR2*. In an article entitled "Catalogers, Cocktails, and Conversation," he listed some of the more entertaining bits of gossip that he managed to overhear when some catalogers got together for drinks and chitchat:

THINGS OVERHEARD AT CATALOGERS' COCKTAIL PARTIES

1. "I'd like you to meet Heloise. She's doing some very interesting things with semicolons."

2. "Then, after I asked myself the question, 'What am I living for — the Serbo-Croatian Cataloging Round Table or me?' I decided that I really couldn't separate the two entities."

3. "Hi, I'd like you to meet Phil. He's sort of the pocket part of my life."

4. "Oh, didn't you hear, Fred died last February. They put a copy of Dewey in his coffin."

5. "Harold and I have been going together for six months but we haven't quite decided if our relationship should still be classified under 'ephemera.'"

6. "The baby arrived last month, but Richard and I still haven't been able to agree if his last name should be 'Snodgrass-Klotz,' 'Snodgrass Klotz,' 'Klotz-Snodgrass,' or 'Klotz Snodgrass.' There really ought to be an *AACR2* manual for naming babies."

7. "I told Agnes that I am a cataloger and that if she wanted more conversation she should have married Ted Koppel."

8. "To me a mixed marriage is when a reference librarian marries a cataloger."

9. "I think I'm in love with Arnold. His main entries are rather unimaginative, but his added entries are very creative, if you know what I mean."

10. "Don't look at your relationship with Bill as a marriage, look at it as a long running serial with daily updates."

11. "My twelve year old son wants to be a big league baseball player but there's still hope for my ten year old daughter. She says that she lives for the day when she can create authority files."

12. "You say Jonathan, your nonfiction cataloger, died? How could you tell?"[12]

Catching snippets of cataloging chitchat might be fun for some, but it's not all that instructive. To expand your knowledge base you might want to take Philip A. Farson's advice and go hang out around the main bar at the conference hotel after midnight. According to Farson, that's when librarians really hunker down and trade professional secrets. In an article entitled "What A.L.A. Has Taught Me," Farson enumerates the following things that he gleaned "just hanging around the bar":

WHAT PHILIP A. FARSON HAS LEARNED AT A.L.A. CONFERENCES

1. How to balance a spoon on his nose.
2. What a B-52 with wings is.
3. How to wiggle his ears.
4. The words to the Georgia Tech fight song.
5. Where the nude beaches in San Diego are located.
6. What PeeWee Herman's real name is.
7. Who played Lumpy Rutherford on "Leave It to Beaver."
8. Which Executive Board members ride in limousines.
9. The real story behind the Linda Crismond firing.
10. The real story behind the death of Melvil Dewey.
11. What prominent male librarians are cross-dressers.
12. What really happened in room 112 in the Hilton during the A.L.A. Midwinter blizzard of 1977.
13. How to play "Yellow Submarine" with a fork and a beer mug.[13]

What other tips do you have for novice conference goers?

1. **Do Not Wear Your Conference Nametag After Dark.** What is the purpose of the conference nametag? Right, it's supposed to identify you and indicate where you are from, which is the last thing you want people to know after dark. The unfortunate reality of American life is that there is not one big city in our country where you are not at risk when you are out walking around at night, even if it is just between the conference center and your hotel. To professional (and amateur) criminals your conference nametag does a wonderful job of identifying you as an easy prey in the urban jungle.

2. **Dress Sensibly and Comfortably.** If you would expect anyone to dress sensibly and comfortably it would be librarians. That's our

image. We dress for comfort rather than style. So you tell me why nine out of every ten people attending the ALA Annual Conference in Dallas persist in wearing wool suits and silk neckties and scarves to conference programs, meetings, and exhibits? Are they trying not to look like librarians? Well, I've got news for them. A wool suit in Dallas in July does not exactly establish professional credibility. In fact, it makes librarians look nerdier than ever.

3. Do Some Strategic Planning. Ordinarily, strategic planning is a useless endeavor pursued by managers with too much time on their hands. JUST DO IT is usually a much better course of action. The exception, of course, is the ALA Conference.

THINGS THAT WILL HAPPEN TO YOU IF YOU DON'T PLAN

A. You will wait forty-five minutes in line at the coffee shop in your hotel for the privilege of paying ten dollars so that you can eat significantly overcooked (or possibly undercooked) eggs for breakfast.

B. You will wait twenty minutes in line at the shuttle bus stop in front of your hotel for the privilege of cramming yourself into a hot, dirty bus with seventy-five other people to take a five minute ride to the convention center.

C. You will wait fifteen minutes in line at the hot dog stand outside the convention center for the privilege of paying four dollars so that you can eat a significantly undercooked (or possibly overcooked) hot dog for your lunch.

D. You will spend two hours aimlessly wandering around the exhibit hall desperate to find someone you know who will be a decent dinner companion (i.e., someone who will not embarrass you by pulling out a calculator to figure out who owes what when the bill arrives).

E. You will finally latch on to a group of reference librarians you vaguely knew from a committee you once served on and go with them to "Interstices," a trendy restaurant recommended by *Library Journal*, where you will find a line of 57 people, most of whom are holding Baker and Taylor shopping bags.

F. After waiting forty-five minutes and progressing to 26th in line, you decide to bail out and grab a cab and head for the McDonald's located down the street from your hotel.

G. After waiting twenty minutes for a cab you finally throw caution to the four winds and decide to walk. After all, you ask yourself, what's the difference between dying of hunger and being mugged?

H. After being followed for four blocks by a man with a scar on his right cheek you duck into a hotel lobby where the desk clerk asks, "How many hours will you need a room?"

I. You get back into the street and are relieved to know that the man with the scar on his right cheek is gone, but twenty minutes later, guess what? You find yourself back in front of Interstices and, guess what? Your party of reference librarians is now first in line.

J. You nonchalantly rejoin them ("Goodness it took forever to get into that bathroom") and five minutes later you're seated at a table next to another table where four people are talking about interlibrary loan fill rates.

K. After waiting for fifty-two minutes your meal, veal Oscar, arrives and it's overcooked, which you tolerate because you're so hungry that you'd eat it even if someone told you that what you are about to eat is a dog named Oscar. Also, the piece of meat they've given you is so small that whether it's undercooked or overcooked is completely academic.

L. Unfortunately not everyone in your party is as tolerant. Two of your dinner mates send their meals back. As a consequence, dinner takes an extra forty-five minutes, and now you find yourself talking about interlibrary loan fill rates.

M. It takes twenty-seven minutes to get a taxi and at 11:00 you find yourself back in front of your hotel, but instead of going up to your room you walk down the street to the McDonald's to get some real food. It's closed.

N. On the way up to your room you run into Kim who just has to buy you a drink and talk about old times.

O. After three drinks, Kim wanders off to the bathroom and never comes back.

P. The waitress comes up to you and says "Last call," and you say, "What the hey, how about a double vodka on the rocks."

Q. The bar tab ($57.23) arrives and you say, "What the hey, charge it to my room."

R. The guy at the piano starts playing "Stormy Weather" and it makes you cry because you realize you are not happy.

S. After everyone else in the lounge has left, you go around to each table and start emptying bowls of pretzels into your pockets.

T. You begin the long trek up to your room but on the way you stop at the front desk where you say, "I need a seven A.M. wake-up call. I have a Social Responsibilities Round Table meeting at eight." The desk clerk says "okay" but looks at you like you're an alien.

U. You make it up to your room and instinctively turn on the television because you're lonely. The movie channel is on. It's that absorbing, frenetic, and awful thing about the life and death of Jim Morrison. Somehow you connect this madness to your own life and you sit on the edge of the bed eating pretzels and watching it for two hours. It is now 4 A.M.

V. While trying to make up your mind about whether or not to take a shower, you fall asleep.

W. At 7 A.M. the phone rings.

X. No problem about making that SRRT meeting. You're already dressed.

Y. You go down to the coffee shop and wait in line for forty-five minutes for the privilege of paying ten dollars so that you can eat significantly overcooked (or possibly undercooked) eggs for breakfast.

Z. You wait twenty minutes in line at the shuttle bus stop for the privilege of cramming yourself into a hot, dirty bus with seventy-five other people to take a five minute ride to the convention center.

What's the absolute last word on ALA conferences?

Watch out for a guy named Ralph. He's an on-line searcher with a nose for money and he hasn't missed an ALA conference in twelve years — only he doesn't go as a librarian. He goes as a panhandler. According to him it's a very lucrative pursuit. At one conference (Chicago in '85) he made almost five hundred dollars after expenses, and he stays at only the finest hotels.

Actually Ralph went to his first ALA conference as an on-line searcher. One night while he was standing out on the sidewalk and waiting for a taxi he noticed how generous his fellow librarians were in giving money to panhandlers. So every year after that Ralph got wise. He took off his on-line searcher hat and put on his poor boy hat, which incidentally is not a real stretch for a librarian to make. He doesn't feel too guilty about this form of moonlighting, because he's used the money to help pay for his daughter's college tuition, and she's studying to be—you guessed it—a librarian. He also says that librarians seem to feel better about themselves after giving to the poor. His motto is: Hookers go to plumbing conventions and panhandlers go to library conferences.

Notes

1. Gerhard Carpmeyer, "Social Activities of Early Man as Depicted in Pre-Historic Cave Drawings," *Journal of Euro-American Anthropology* (December 1989) 567.

2. Helena Figtower, *Guilty by Association: Why Librarians Love to Join Professional Organizations* (Providence: Bookpeople Press, 1993), p. 47.

3. *Ibid.*, p. 52.

4. Itinia Needleman, "Good Things About Bad Organizations and Bad Things About Good Organizations," *Library World* (May 1991) 15.

5. *Ibid.*, 21.

6. Sylvia Abbott Hines, "Library Association Involvement: Getting in Too Deep," *The Contemporary Librarian* (September 1991) 87.

7. Harland Bodan Falkner, "I Love My Wife But She Could Make Some Improvements—The Same Goes for A.L.A," *The Irrepressible Librarian* (August 1992) 23.

8. Edna O. Westby, "I Joined A.L.A. to Get the Paul Newman READ Poster," *Library Lifelines* (April 1990) 63.

9. Herbert Whitehead Westmoreland, "Hey ALA, Do You Think You Could Do Something About the Hole in the Ozone?" *The Irrepressible Librarian* (February 1991) 79.

10. Michael D. Unseld, "Librarians Who Need Librarians Are the Luckiest Librarians in the World," *New Age Librarian* (July 1992) 222.

11. Frank Slocum, *Bibliospeak* (Erie: Ampersand Publications, 1989), pp. 52–53.

12. Edward W.S. Weintraub, "Catalogers, Cocktails, and Conversation," *Library World* (October 1992) 17–19.

13. Philip A. Farson, "What A.L.A. Has Taught Me," *Library Weekly* (June 27, 1991) 14.

IMAGE

Hey babe, I'm a librarian. *GQ* says we're what's happening in the 90s.

What is the stereotypical image of the American librarian?

Stern, efficient, and humorless or in Jerry Holley's words, "Did you hear about the librarian with twenty-three different personalities? They're all boring." Comedian Cyd Siricca may have been even more cutting when he joked, "How do librarians have foreplay? They lie in bed and read how-to books."

Is this necessarily a bad image?

Not comparatively speaking. Librarians actually have a better stereotype than many other vocational types. Lawyers, politicians, plumbers, flight attendants, savings and loan presidents, stock brokers, car salesmen, assembly line workers, and construction workers (just to name a few) all have less flattering stereotypes. While librarians are seen as overly serious, that is certainly preferable to being seen as dishonest, greedy, lazy, violent, or stupid.

Why then are librarians so constantly restless and upset about their image?

Because librarians *are* overly serious. It hurts us to have others poke fun at our fussbudget ways, and this, according to Dr. Emily Shoemaker, the noted psychologist who has done numerous studies into the psychological impact of vocational stereotypes, simply reinforces the common perception that we are humorless. Instead of simply laughing off the stereotype we sit and stew about it. Shoemaker writes, "The more librarians quarrel and complain about their stereotype, the more they become their stereotype."[1]

Furthermore, Shoemaker contends that to have a stereotype, even one that is not completely flattering, is actually a very positive development. "People deal with reality," she writes, "by creating stereotypes. If you stereotype something you can understand it or at least pretend to understand it. Stereotyping is how we bring order to our everyday lives."[2] Her ultimate point is that to be stereotyped is to be accepted as a part of reality. "Those professions that should be concerned about their image are the ones who have no stereotype. If you are not stereotyped you are not recognized. To be important is to be stereotyped, and to be stereotyped is to be important."[3]

Dr. Alfred A. Praddle, author of the bestseller *Reality Is Perception and Perception Is Reality,* makes a similar point when he writes, "A nickname, unlike a formal name, is a type of stereotype. We would expect someone who has been given the nickname, 'Iron Mike,' to be a tough, uncompromising individual. People tend to relish their nicknames because to have a nickname means you stand out, that you are worthy of special mention, even if the nickname carries with it a partially negative message."[4] He also makes the interesting point that people without nicknames will sometimes succumb to the humiliating temptation of trying to give themselves a nickname, but that always fails. In Praddle's words, "You can no more nickname yourself than you can chew your own teeth, and the same goes for stereotyping."[5]

Therefore should librarians stop trying to change their image and accept their stereotype with a mixture of grace, humor and even flattery?

The anthropologist F. Sterling Buckingham, in his book *Wishes, Dreams, Myths, and Stereotypes,* argues that we need to understand that stereotypes are more than just a means of classifying, describing, and coming to terms with the disparate elements that exist in our complex world. To him stereotyping is a form of wish projection. Our stereotypes represent how we want a particular person to behave. In Buckingham's words, "stereotypes are molds that we expect people to fit into."[6]

He asks, "What kind of person do we want to have as our accountant? Who do we want handling our money? We want someone who is trustworthy, conservative, exact, and, yes, boring. A flamboyant accountant would make us very nervous. Therefore we construct a stereotype of an accountant—trustworthy, conservative, exacting, and boring—that fits our needs and wishes, and we expect all accountants to conform to that stereotype. The same holds true for lawyers. Our stereotype for lawyers—the rapacious, slick, predatory barracuda—exists because that's the type of person we want on our side when we're in deep trouble. We don't want someone polite and passive; we want someone shrewd, powerful, and even a bit ruthless. And when it comes to undertakers the last thing we want is funny. Funny is definitely not funny when it comes to funerals."[7]

That is why, in Buckingham's opinion, it is completely futile for professionals to try to willfully alter their stereotype. In his mind it simply can't be done. The librarian stereotype exists because that is the personality mold that society wants librarians to conform to. Society sees the library as a quiet place with a serious purpose. It should be staffed, therefore, by quiet and serious people.

While willing to entertain Buckingham's premise that stereotypes are collective wish projections, noted librarian-activist Amelia Stansberry is completely unwilling to accept his conclusion that librarians have some kind of societal obligation to conform to that stereotype. She writes, "Should blacks conform to the stereotypes that whites have burdened them with? Should women submit to stereotypes given to them by men? Of course not, and furthermore, librarians should not accept their stereotypes."[8] It is Stansberry's strong belief that stereotypes are cages that the power elite use to control people, professions, and institutions.

How can librarians most effectively rebel against their stereotype?

Image patrols, boycotts, legal threats, counterinsults, and dress for success workshops will not work according to Rebecca Barrows-Brown, professor of librarianship at the Fogbottom School of Information Science. She feels very strongly that if we go to war with the world about our image we will simply confirm everyone's worst suspicions that we are stern, strict, and humorless.

Barrows-Brown did a study of how 18 different professional groups, from shoe salesmen to gynecologists, react to their stereotypical image. Her research centered on scrutinizing the contents of the professional literature of each of the professional groups, and her findings were quite revealing. She discovered that in the five year period from 1987 to 1992 there were more articles dealing with image in the three major library trade journals than in all of the other professional trade journals put together. While others don't seem to worry about their image, librarians are in a constant state of rebellion about theirs. Barrows-Brown concludes that despite these efforts, the image of librarians did not change appreciably in that five year period.[9]

If rebellion is not the answer, what is?

Helter-skelter. In a much talked about *Library Monthly* article entitled "Media Masquerade: Getting Ahead of the Image Curve," William Sedgewick, director of the Rockbound (Maine) Public Library, argues that if librarians want to change their image, they can only do it by exploiting the mass media. In this article (which some people say is actually an outrageous parody), Sedgewick says that librarians need to get into the mass media in a way that is completely at odds with the standard stereotype. He thinks that librarians need to impact all the popular media outlets that shape the views and opinions of the American people, and puts forth what he calls "prototypes" for doing this. Listed below are a series of possibilities that Sedgewick feels would do more to change how people feel about librarians than all the litigation in the world.

THE WORLD ACCORDING TO WILLIAM SEDGEWICK

Tabloid Headlines
> "Caveman Returns Library Book 20,000 Years Overdue"
> "Psycho Librarian Stalks Problem Patrons in Cleveland: Death
> Toll 57"
> "Boston Cataloger Gives Birth to 20 Pound Rutabaga"
> "Michael Landon Spotted Reading His Obituaries in Microfilm
> Room of Beverly Hills Public Library"

Soap Opera Listings
> "Santa Barbara Public Library"
> "All My Librarians"
> "Young Catalogers in Love"

Movie Titles
> "The Circ Staff from Hell"
> "Cataloger's Revenge: Library Chain Saw Massacre Part 2"
> "I Love It When You Talk Dewey to Me" (X rated)
> "Cathy Does Cataloging" (XXX rated)

Television Talk Show Topics
> "Librarians Who Love Too Much"
> "Catalogers Who Have Turned into Dogs"
> "Bibliographers Who Molested Their Parents"
> "Librarians Who Had Affairs with JFK"

Rap Songs
> "Cataloger Killer"

"White Librarians Can't Dance"
"The Drag Queen of O.C.L.C."
Bumper Stickers
"Honk If You Love Your Librarian"
"Save Original Catalogers from Extinction"
"Have You Hugged Your Circ Clerk Today?"
Video Games
"Super Mario Brothers, Level 4: Loose in the Library of Congress"
"Donkey Kong Does Boolean Searching"[10]

Doesn't Sedgewick's approach really substitute one bad image for another?

Actually Sedgewick's "helter-skelter" approach is based on the premise that librarians are too varied and unpredictable to stereotype. His hope is that through his recommended media assault, librarians will be incapable of being branded by any kind of an image. In that scenario the unique characteristics of each librarian will shine through.

Carlton Carmody, a well known library consultant specializing in the marketing of public sector services, agrees with Sedgewick that a "no image" strategy is ultimately in the profession's best interest, but he thinks that it is naive for Sedgewick to believe that Hollywood would have any interest at all in featuring libraries and librarians in their entertainment productions. In an article entitled "Image Makeover in 365 Days," he writes, "The recent recession has dealt a fatal blow to Hollywood's proclivity to experiment with new themes and characters. Investors are simply unwilling to risk their money on Sedgewick's idea that librarians will suddenly become nouveau-chic once their more latent idiosyncrasies are revealed."[11]

He, therefore, advocates that libraries concentrate their diversity and unpredictability on a more local stage. Special events and special programming are the keys by which librarians can attract attention locally but only if they are willing to exercise their creativity and take risks. The standard, unimaginative programs on decorating Christmas trees and wrapping Christmas presents simply will not do the trick. Instead Carmody suggests that librarians follow his twelve "image enhancing program ideas":

CARLTON CARMODY'S YEAR
ROUND IMAGE ENHANCERS

1. January — Gender Consciousness Raising Month. This is a great way to start the new year. Men need to have a better understanding of what it is like to be female in America, and women need to begin to develop a feel for how difficult it is for men to be seen as sensitive and not wimpy. Suggested activities include a cross-dressing exercise in which male librarians dress up as women and the female librarians dress up as males, so that everyone gets a first hand opportunity to experience how the opposite gender is treated by the public.

2. February — Kill a Lawyer Month. What better way to spend this cold, cruel month than to cash in on America's love of hating lawyers. Talk about an image problem, the lawyers have the worst. In the eyes of the public, lawyers are lower than undertakers, used car salesmen, and even politicians. What librarians should do, therefore, is publicize books (the big bestseller *The Firm* is a good example) that illustrate the growing trend among American authors to follow Shakespeare's advice and kill off all the lawyers (purely in a literary sense, of course).

3. March — Everyone Is Pregnant Month. Everyone has rights but pregnant women. There ought to be a law, for instance, that libraries cannot keep books on pregnancy on the bottom shelf where it is impossible for pregnant women to access them. But in most libraries where do you find the books on pregnancy? That's right. You find them on the bottom shelf. Every librarian, therefore, should willingly go through the entire month of March wearing one of those fake pregnancy devices. By April I guarantee there won't be *any* books shelved on the bottom shelf.

4. April — Trick the I.R.S. Month. April means one thing to most public services librarians: distributing tax forms. And for this effort what do we get? Well, for one thing we never get any thanks from the I.R.S., and for another thing we never get any thanks from our patrons. In fact we get their anger because they think we *are* the I.R.S. So here's what we do to get a little attention: we give out fake forms with significantly reduced tax rates. Oh don't worry about getting locked up. The I.R.S. has a sense of humor, especially when it comes to April Fools' jokes. Not.

5. May — Dress Like a Librarian Month. Speaking of a sense of humor nothing establishes your own sense of humor better than your ability to laugh at yourself. Remember all those dumb blonde jokes that were going around a few years ago? I've got news for you, the blondes who reacted to those jokes with wit and humor, gained respect, but those who responded with petulance, simply reinforced their superficial, pea-brained stereotype. What could be more fun for librarians than to dress up like librarians—you know, the tight hair in a bun, pencils sticking out of the hair, wire rimmed spectacles, a shawl, clunky shoes, plastic pocket protectors, and mismatched socks. Not only would this establish our sense of irony, it would also show demonstrably that we ordinarily do *not* dress like librarians.

6. June—Swimsuit Month. What could be funnier than to follow up a month of shawls and specs with a month of swimsuits and beach towels. No one would ever call us shy or retiring again. The public would love us. In fact, the part that they would love the most would be not just that we have a sense of daring that borders on the absurd, but that it is actually very reassuring to see normal people in swimsuits rather than the models that you see in magazines.

7. July—Crips and Bloods Month. Okay, it's the middle of summer. You've got lots of leisure time on your hands and the hot weather is making you a bit testy. Now's the time to break out the latest in gang attire. No, don't do anything violent but just let everyone in your hood get a glimpse of your darker side. A little leather and a leg tattoo would help. After all, fun's fun but we do want to be taken seriously too.

8. August—Turn the Library into Tahiti Month. Did you ever stop to think about all the people who can't afford to take a vacation? These days folks feel good if they get the rent paid on time let alone pile the kids in the car and head off to Vacationland. So turn your library into a resort. One year do Tahiti, the next year scale Mt. Everest. Actually when all is said and done there's no better place to spend a little leisure time than at the library with a bunch of wild and crazy librarians. Make it happen.

9. September—Football Month. Whose image is the direct opposite of the librarian's? That's easy. It's the professional football player. Loud, obnoxious, violent, bulky, rich, and revered, your average middle linebacker is seen as being everything that your average Slavic language cataloger is not. So why not split the library staff into two teams and kick off the season with a friendly but ferocious game of tackle football on the library's front lawn? But first you'd better make sure those health insurance premiums are paid in full.

10. October—Throw a BYOCS (Bring Your Own Chain Saw) Party. One of America's greatest gifts to literature is the horror genre. It all started back in the late eighteenth century with the gothic novels of Charles Brockden Brown and has progressed nicely through the short stories of Edgar Allan Poe and Ambrose Bierce culminating today in the thrillers of Stephen King. In fact, the slasher genre is so legit it has even found a niche in young adult literature with the works of Christopher Pike. The truth is we Americans love to be terrified. We can't get enough of it. So join the fun. This Halloween throw a BYOCS party in your library, and celebrate our great American literary tradition.

11. November—A.B.T. (Anything But Turkey) Month. It's hard to think of a better holiday than Thanksgiving. It celebrates our cultural diversity, it cuts across all religious, ethnic, and racial lines, it does not involve expensive gift giving, you get the day off from work, and the main focus is food. Think about it: we are lucky enough to have a day that is basically devoted to eating, a day in which it would be unpatriotic to diet. And so what do we do with the day? We eat turkey—tough, stringy, tasteless turkey. This makes no sense. There are about nine hundred foods that are more fun to eat than turkey. We all know that but very few Americans are willing to take the social risks involved with serving something other than turkey for Thanksgiving dinner. That's why librarians can make a difference by promoting the concept of a turkey-free Thanksgiving holiday. Cookbooks featuring alternative menus could be highlighted, and programs instructing people in the fine art of preparing lobster could be provided. Believe me, America is just waiting for someone to have the guts to break with tradition, and declare that only turkeys eat turkey for Thanksgiving.

12. December—Do Nothing Month. That's right, forget the Christmas tree, the Santa Claus imitators, the jingle bells, the partridges in pear trees, the boughs of holly, the mistletoe, the lights, the candles, the reindeer horns, and the visions of sugarplums. There's enough of that at home, in the mall, and on the streets. Holiday cheer is so pervasive that it's getting to be too much. People need a break from all that. There's where the library can provide a real holiday service. By resisting the temptation to deck the halls, librarians can provide weary Americans a much needed break from holiday hoopla. And who knows? Maybe in our bare reading rooms people will actually be able to reflect on the reason for the season. As they say in architecture, "less is more."[12]

Do you really expect anyone to follow Carmody's recommendations?

No, not completely. America is not yet ready for Carlton Carmody for the simple reason that America is becoming more conservative. What I think we librarians should do is to start taking some of the observations of Gertrude Mustard Strong more seriously. Despite the fact that her article "I've Got My Gray Hair in a Bun and There's No Way in Hell I'm Getting It Frosted!" was widely criticized in the library profession for reinforcing old stereotypes, in all fairness you have to admit that Mustard Strong makes some rather interesting points.

Basically she argues that baby boomers are aging and are therefore becoming more oriented toward health, fitness, and family. In short, boomers are becoming sensible, to the point of almost being stuffy. Does that sound a little like the stereotypical image of the librarian? That's exactly Mustard Strong's point. Librarians are becoming as fashionable as Birkenstocks and oat bran. There's no need, therefore, to change our image. We are what is happening in America. Everyone wants to be like us.[13]

Don't get me wrong. I don't think that we'll ever become so fashionable that you'll be sitting on an airplane and suddenly hear a voice over the loud speaker asking, "Is there a librarian on the plane? Mr. Armondy in the front row is restless. He needs something good to read." And I don't think in time of war that the head of your draft board will call you up and say, "We're not going to draft you because we've decided that librarians are too valuable here at home."

But still the trend is obvious: America is coming our way.

That does nothing, however, for our money problem. Isn't it true that to make more money we have to create a more powerful image for ourselves?

Remember, this is the 90s. The starched white shirts, yellow ties, and red suspenders of the greedy 80s are over. Rich is no longer chic. Middle class is where it's at today. In fact people realize they're lucky *not* to be rich. Think of all the advantages. In an article entitled "I Only Know One Rich Person Who Is Happy and He Got Run Over by His Own Limousine and Died," Robert Rogerson writes that when you are poor you don't have to worry about:

1. Buying a vacation home in Cannes and finding out six weeks later that all of the beautiful people have suddenly decided that Monte Carlo is the place to dock your yacht.

2. Finding a mechanic who knows something about the insides of a Mercedes Benz.

3. Having someone marry you for your money.

4. Being ripped off by high-priced financial advisors.

5. Watching your Malibu beach house being destroyed by an earthquake, mudslide, tidal wave, or race riot.

6. Losing a million dollar diamond brooch in a dish full of caviar.

7. Finding someone responsible to pilot your private jet.

8. Getting dinged by the new federal taxes when purchasing a new yacht.

9. Finding legal tax shelters for millions of dollars.

10. Picking the right psychiatrist for your dog.

11. Getting spaghetti stains on a $200 handpainted Italian necktie.

12. Getting lost in the woods during a fox hunt.

13. Figuring out the rules of polo.

14. Choking on a piece of French truffle.

15. Trying to find racially diverse members for your exclusive country club.[14]

What's the final word on the image issue?

If you don't like the librarian's image, go to law school.

Notes

1. Emily Shoemaker, "I Am Stereotyped Therefore I Am," *Today's Librarian* (November 1987) 59.

2. *Ibid.*, 62.

3. *Ibid.*, 63.

4. Alfred Alan Praddle, *Reality Is Perception and Perception Is Reality* (New York: Torkleson Books, 1985), p. 193.

5. *Ibid.*, p. 194.

6. Ferdinand Sterling Buckingham, *Wishes, Dreams, Myths, and Stereotypes* (Los Angeles: Reality Press, 1989), p. 78.

7. *Ibid.*, p. 197.

8. Amelia Stansberry, "How the Power Elite Uses Stereotypes to Control Society," *The Socially Responsible Librarian* (winter 1989) 93.

9. Rebecca Barrows-Brown, "Image Obsession: A Comparative Study," *Library Review* (spring 1993) 38–57.

10. William Sedgewick, "Media Masquerade: Getting Ahead of the Image Curve," *Library Monthly* (April 1993) 65–73.

11. Carlton Carmody, "Image Makeover in 365 Days," *The Contemporary Librarian* (June 1993) 38.

12. *Ibid.*, 40–51.

13. Gertrude Mustard Strong, "I've Got My Gray Hair in a Bun and There's No Way in Hell I'm Getting It Frosted!" *The Irrepressible Librarian* (August 1992) 33–34. This veteran librarian created a great fuss with this article. Many younger librarians attacked it for "reinforcing undesirable stereotypes." A good example of this criticism is the article "Buns Are Something You Eat." It was written by Heather Hunter McQuaid and it appeared in the January 1993 issue of *Today's Librarian*.

14. Robert Rogerson, "I Only Know One Rich Person Who Is Happy and He Got Run Over by His Own Limousine and Died," *Plain Folks* (April 21, 1992) 13–15.

GETTING A DEGREE
&
GETTING A JOB

I know $19,500 isn't much but didn't they tell you in library school that M.L.S. stands for "Makes Low Salary?"

Do librarians really need to have a master's degree in library science?

First of all, library science is an oxymoron. There is absolutely nothing scientific about librarianship. Where, for instance, does the "scientific method" come into play in librarianship and when is the last time you heard someone refer to himself as a library scientist? Librarianship is about people and there's nothing scientific about people. Where's the science in dealing with a confused ten year old, a demanding college student, a frantic parent, an imperious scholar, a purple-headed skateboarder, or a two-year-old who toddles up to you and pees on your sock?

The point is that librarianship is an art, and if the library profession really wants to have a professional degree it should be an M.A.L.—master of arts in librarianship. Those who want to become scientists should head for the chemistry department.

Isn't the difference between an M.L.S. and an M.A.L. simply semantic?

Absolutely not. The distinction between science and art couldn't be more stark. Scientists compute, artists create; scientists analyze, artists intuit; scientists experiment, artists take risks; scientists are objective, artists are subjective; scientists evaluate, artists make value judgments; scientists hug the shore of physical reality, artists venture out into the deep sea of the metaphysical; scientists love uniformity, artists love originality; scientists wear white lab coats, artists wear smocks. The M.L.S. encourages conformity, standardization, and normative procedures.

What does all of this mean when it comes to libraries?

In short, library school should develop creative thinkers. That's the message of Timothy A. Toomer, director of the Alexander A. Buttersworth Memorial Library. In an article entitled "Measuring a Job Candidate's Creativity Quotient," Toomer describes a very unorthodox testing technique that he utilizes as part of his interviewing process. During the middle of a job interview he gets up and says, "Please excuse me I have a very important phone call to make." Then he hands the job candidate a new Lego box and says "Here's something to keep you busy while I'm gone." Then he leaves the room for twenty minutes.

What's the method in this madness? Very simple. Lego blocks are little pieces of plastic that come in a diverse array of sizes and shapes—rectangular, curvilinear, and even triangular—and in every Lego box you will find blueprints for any number of structures— houses, airplane hangars, and even space stations.

According to Toomer, "If you're a conventional person, someone who obediently does whatever you are told to do by an authority figure, you will meticulously follow the designs prescribed in the Lego blueprints. But if you are a creative person you will rip the box open and either ignore the blueprints or more probably lose them. The real challenge of Lego is not to follow directions but to build something imaginative and innovative, something that no one else has ever done before."[1]

So when Toomer returns to the interviewing room he checks to see what the candidate has done with the box of Legos. If the candidate has either not opened the box at all or has opened the box and simply followed the canned instructions, he or she will not get the job.

Toomer claims that "the challenge of librarianship is actually rather similar to Lego building. As professionals, our charge is not to do what everybody else is doing but to develop a library that is tailored to the unique community that supports it. This is the great fun of librarianship. Our communities form a tapestry of diversity. There are over fifty thousand different libraries in the United States serving communities as different as the Harvard Divinity School and the little village of Strawberry Plains, Tennessee. Within this spectrum the opportunity for creativity is unlimited. Unfortunately, however, too many librarians are like the proverbial obedient child who simply follows the prescribed instructions that come with the Lego box. This ingrained sense of conformity is ironic because of the library profession's deep commitment to the principles of intellectual freedom. Librarians oddly enough are the first to defend the ideal of intellectual freedom and the last to exercise it. Next to the words 'we've always done it that way,' the phrase 'everybody is doing it' is the most common explanation that librarians give for putting their Lego blocks together in the predictable way that they do."[2]

How can library school promote independent thinking?

In picking up on Toomer's comment, the first thing library schools should do is to present intellectual freedom not only as a concept to defend, but as a concept to exercise! Right now, however, library school curriculums encourage conformity, not creativity.

In his scathing essay "The Library School Gulag," Sidney A. Bold claims that the big problem with most library schools is that they get too bogged down in procedural details. He writes, "Library educators need to begin developing a grand unified theory of librarianship, because without this theory library education amounts to nothing much more than the kind of practical vocational training that you find in the average trade school, where a student learns an occupational bag of tricks."[3]

A good place to start developing this theory would be with a reconsideration of some of the works of Ridley Finn. Granted, most libraries (and library schools) have probably weeded many of Finn's titles. They are after all thirty to forty years old. But curiously they're not out of date. In fact, they are rather relevant to the identity crisis that library education is suffering from today. Far from being seen as an art, librarianship today (as seen by the library academic establishment) is being dished out more and more as a science and not just as library science but as information science (which certainly sounds more scientific than library science).

That is why Finn is so important. He reminds us of why civilizations choose to build and support libraries: not just to provide books and information but more importantly to act as a kind of bulwark of civilization reminding humankind not only of its dreams and aspirations but also of its possibilities. In other words the idea of a library is just as important to us as the library itself. He put it this way: "Even if God doesn't exist, the idea of God is a tremendously civilizing notion, especially if our image of God is a civilizing one."[4] In Finn's view the implacable power of Christianity lies in its concept of God. That the Christian God of love would supplant the Old Testament God of anger or the Roman gods of whim was inevitable because a civilized people quite naturally prefer love and forgiveness to anger, revenge, and capriciousness. In Finn's view, therefore, it is not enough simply to have a library. The library must also serve the purposes of civilization if it is to grow, thrive, and develop, and for Finn the basis of civilization is leisure, for leisure is what gives us the opportunity to engage in philosophical introspection, and philosophical introspection is what separates men and women from the rest of the animal kingdom. If the library is to be relevant, therefore, it must be able to support our restless search for meaning. It is highly ironic that in 1947 Finn saw the worship of work as a threat to the pursuit of philosophy. So strong was the work ethic in the post–World War II era, that work itself became the meaning of life, and Finn's main contribution to the literature of librarianship was to warn against the danger that this doctrine of pragmatism posed to the theory of librarianship.

Finn's body of work is particularly important if you buy into some of the more trenchant social observations of Dr. Andover Oppenheimer. In an article entitled "The Truth About the Home Computer," he demonstrates quite forcefully that the main use of the computer is not to access or process information but to play games. If Finn were alive today, therefore, he would no doubt point out the irony that his concept of leisure is threatened more by leisure itself than by work, quickly adding that in contemporary America leisure has more to do with the pursuit of pleasure than the search for meaning. As Oppenheimer has pointed out, our age is not the age of information but rather the age of entertainment. Celebrities are our gods, television is our nationally accepted drug of choice, and Hollywood movies are our most sought after export.[5]

All of this means that if we accept Finn's notion that the library exists as a bulwark of civilization it becomes even more important at times when civilization begins to unravel. It seems to me that a good part of a librarian's education should be creatively exploring the linkages between libraries and civilization and understanding the basic symbiosis of the relationship between the two. Libraries need civilization; and civilization needs libraries. Try to imagine how differently Western civilization would have developed were it not for the Alexandrian Library or the monastic libraries of the Dark Ages.

Is civilization as we know it worth supporting?

It is true, as Sir Brookmeyer Clubbs has written, that "civilization often produces some rather uncivilized results."[6] In his nine volume masterpiece, *The Shibboleths of Civilization: A Multicultural Approach to Human Structures, Values, and Myths,* Clubbs makes the point that civilization—from the invention of the flint arrowhead to the development of the atomic bomb—has often provided man the resources and the organizational capacity to create the most barbaric of circumstances. "History," in the words of Sir Brookmeyer, "is a darkling tale of dishonor."[7]

While one cannot do anything but deplore the details of Clubbs' nine volume tale of woe, one can also take an inner delight in the byproducts of civilization that Clubbs never brings up. This is a point that Dr. Stanley Bridgehopper emphasizes in his book *The Silver Linings of History.* Yes, the Hundred Years War was a long war, but it did provide Shakespeare with some great material. Yes, Hitler was a terrible man, but he gave new life to the field of moral theology. And yes, the development of rocket science has resulted in some pretty destructive weapons, but, hey, teflon isn't a bad spin-off.[8]

While Bridgehopper's optimism seems to know no limits, the truth is that he is on to something. Who among us cannot find at least five things that make life worth living and that affirm the value of civilization. As an example here are my five things:

FIVE THINGS THAT AFFIRM THE VALUE OF CIVILIZATION

1. *Ben and Jerry's Ice Cream.* This falls under the heading of the celebration of the divine and just beats out the Cathedral at Chartres for the honor of being the one thing on earth that gives us our best sense of paradise. You simply cannot deny the existence of God or the concept of heaven after eating Ben and Jerry's ice cream. No, it doesn't make up for Hitler, but as Sinatra says: "whatever gets you through the night. . . ."

2. *The National Enquirer.* It's a wonderful concept that these tabloid people have come up with. They have created a publication that puts everyman's life into perspective. You may be depressed that you're not rich and famous, but me, I don't have that problem. I read the *National Enquirer,* and that is all I need to be fulfilled in my modest little life as a librarian. How lucky I feel that (a) I am not a mass murderer, (b) I don't have any mysterious diseases, and (c) my son has not given birth to a chimpanzee in the Philippines. You can take drugs for your depression, I'll read the N.E.

3. *The V.C.R.* Every civilization has its bread and circuses. Ours

is football. Last Saturday there were five football games on television. Since the average length of a football game is three hours, to see all three games I would have had to make an investment of fifteen hours. But with my VCR I can tape each game and shrink the viewing time to fourteen minutes by fast forwarding through huddles and commercials. That leaves plenty of time for Plato, Aristotle, and Aquinas.

4. *Deodorant.* If, as Ridley Finn has written, man's search for meaning ultimately leads to a struggle to transcend our animalistic impulses and develop our spiritual sensibilities, then deodorant should be right up there with the Dead Sea Scrolls as an uplifting resource. After all, it's hard to think of a man having a soul when he smells like a monkey.

5. *The Sneaker.* Be honest, don't your sneakers make you feel happy to be alive. They're comfortable, practical, versatile, and attractive all at the same time — something that you can say about no other form of footwear. And the variety is mindboggling. In judging past civilizations it's easy to be critical, but we should always keep in mind that they did not have the benefit of the sneaker.

To point out these pleasures of civilization, of course, is not to say that I see the world through rose colored glasses. There is a lot about civilization that in my opinion we can take no pride in. What follows is a list of some of those things:

THREE BAD THINGS ABOUT CIVILIZATION

1. *Polyester.* Do you realize that those polyester pants that you bought twenty years ago will take over 20,000 years to disintegrate? Maybe that's why so many people are being buried in polyester leisure suits. As an experiment, take a minute and look through your family album. I am sure that you will find that appearance-wise you look your worst in the pictures from the 1970s. There's a reason for that. You were probably dressed in polyester. The 60s may have been about freedom and the 80s may have been about wealth, but the 70s were definitely about polyester, the miracle fabric that made you feel like an oil slick in the summer and a sheet of ice in the winter.

2. *The Discovery of Cholesterol.* The discovery of the link between cholesterol and heart disease has ruined many lives because it has scared us into thinking more about the quantity of life rather than the quality of life. Here's a question for you: Would you rather be happy

and live to be 55 or be unhappy and live to be 85? Personally I'll take happy and 55. My assumption of course is that happiness, true long-term happiness, cannot be achieved with a low fat, low cholesterol diet. Unfortunately, many people today are willing to do anything to stay alive—including eating lettuce three times a day. These people often end up committing suicide. How's that for irony?

3. *The Invention of the Wheel*. The invention of the wheel is unfortunate because it led to the invention of the exercise bicycle. Three years ago I bought a very expensive (the one with the electronic heart monitor) exercise bike—everybody was doing it—and I have been ridden with guilt ever since—probably because I have been on it for a grand total of fifty-seven minutes. It sits in my garage gathering dust. I pass it at least nine or ten times a day. It is too expensive to sell in a garage sale. I often keep my garage door open in hopes that someone will steal it and allow me to at least collect on my insurance policy, but apparently no one else wants it either. Take it from me, if you're going to buy exercise equipment that you probably won't use, buy something cheap like an aerobics step.

If library schools are not immersing students into the larger philosophical questions regarding the nature of civilization, what are they doing?

The conventional criticism about library schools is that they are not practical enough. Many of the students who attend library school and who already work in libraries are usually in the forefront of this criticism. They want their professors to be more "real world" oriented.

My view is the opposite. Library school should actually be less "real world" related. It should be a place given to reflecting, dreaming, visioning, and reinventing. It needs to be more theoretical and less practical.

Unfortunately, however, today's library schools have all the soul of an auto mechanics school. They are process driven not substance driven. They are glorified "how to" schools, not "what" or "why" schools. This is how you order a book. This is how you access a data base. This is how you do on-line cataloging. Today's library education consists of teaching students how to respond to day-to-day dilemmas. It does not inspire them with any sense of how to shape the library into something more than a depository of informational and recreational resources for an existing clientele group. They do not challenge students to engage in the kind of big picture thought about civilization that results in the creative process of rethinking the role of libraries. They've completely ignored the vision thing.

What other problems do you see with library education?

Quite simply that it is not accessible to millions of Americans, and for a profession that espouses openness and accessibility this goes beyond irony to hypocrisy. In an article entitled "Geography 101: In Search of an A.L.A. Accredited Library School," Nancy Rae Studebaker points out that "it is harder to become a librarian than it is a doctor or a lawyer."[9] Her point, of course, has nothing to do with the relative entrance requirements of the three professions and everything to do with the fact that while there are 121 AMA accredited medical schools and 175 ABA accredited law schools there are only 50 ALA accredited library schools.

It is important to note that Nancy Rae Studebaker is a resident of Denver, Colorado. You've probably heard of Denver. It is the center of a metropolitan area of over two million people. There is no ALA accredited library school in Denver. This means that if any of those two million people (such as Nancy Rae Studebaker) want to be librarians they have to pick up stakes and move 1,600 miles southwest to Tucson, Arizona (University of Arizona), 2,000 miles west to Berkeley, California, 1,000 miles east to Emporia, Kansas (Emporia State University), or 1,300 miles southeast to Denton, Texas (Texas Woman's University and University of North Texas).

Nancy Rae Studebaker put her dilemma this way. "Sure I wanted to be a librarian, and yes I even looked forward to going to library science classes, but when I found out that the closest route to becoming a librarian ran through Berkeley, Denton, Tucson, or Emporia, I began looking for another profession. At the time I was thirty years old, the mother of a five year old son and a seven year old daughter, and the wife of an aerospace engineer. Did I want to pay $20,000 for the privilege of moving away and ruining my family, in hopes of eventually getting a job as a reference librarian that would probably pay me $26,000? I hope I don't look that retarded."[10]

The problem is that Nancy Rae Studebaker is not an isolated case study. Nancy Rae would have the same problem if she lived in many other cities or states. For example people who live in Minnesota, Virginia, Wyoming, Oregon, New Mexico, North Dakota, South Dakota, Arkansas, Colorado, Las Vegas, Phoenix, Miami, Memphis, New Orleans, Cleveland, Cincinnati, and Salt Lake City (among many other places) are not within commuting distance to a library school.

In his article "So You Want to Be a Librarian," Philip Thistlewaits calculates that there are 137,456,321 Americans who do not live within commuting distance of a library school, but he is quick to add that none of these people live in Denton (population 66,000) where there are two ALA accredited library schools (Texas Woman's and North Texas). Thistlewaits further calculates that in America there is one library school for every half million people, but in Denton, Texas, there is one library school for every 33,000 residents. Thistlewaits warns prospective librarians that Denton, Texas, is a particularly difficult place to get a job since two out of every ten people there have an M.L.S. He also warns that there is no city in the country where you have a greater chance of having a cataloging professor as your next door neighbor. Finally, he poses the question, "What real man wants a library degree from Texas Woman's University?"[11]

Further on in the article, Thistlewaits raises the issue of what considerations a prospective M.L.S. seeker should keep in mind before making a final decision about whether or not to matriculate in an ALA accredited graduate library program. These are his arguments pro and con:

FIVE GOOD REASONS NOT TO GO TO LIBRARY SCHOOL

1. You still have to take Cataloging.

2. You will spend anywhere from $10,000 to $30,000 to get a degree that will qualify you for a starting job that pays between $18,000 and $22,000.

3. Most of the students in library school actually work in libraries and therefore know more about librarianship than their professors.

4. When you finally get your M.L.S. people will say, "I didn't know you were going to real estate school."

5. The lack of available men can be a deterrent to an active social life.

SIX GOOD REASONS TO GO TO LIBRARY SCHOOL

1. Although the lack of available men can be a deterrent to an active social life, there's nothing to do in Denton, Texas, anyway.

2. You can be 45 and not feel old in library school.

3. A pulse rate is all you need to pass most library science courses (they need your tuition money).

4. On a daily basis the antisocial behavior of your cataloging professors will give you a valuable illustration of how not to deal with library patrons.

5. You get to examine a diverse array of pornographic materials under the rationalization that you are doing research for your intellectual freedom class.

6. After you finish library school and find out that you can't make a decent living as a librarian, having an M.L.S. degree will not hurt your chances of getting into a good x-ray technology school.

What is the best advice that you can give someone who has made the decision to enroll in a graduate school of library science?

Grover C. Littleman, in an article entitled "I Survived Library School and You Can Too," claims that the key to making library school a positive experience is choosing the right professors. He says there are two types of professors. The first type of professor is Professor God. According to Littleman, "it is easy to understand why many professors develop a God complex. When you have complete control over a bunch of people who write down your every thought it is easy to think of yourself in terms of the Godly attributes of omnipotence and omniscience."[12] The second type of professor is Professor Pal. This person is not much happier about being in library school than the student is and so he or she tries to be reasonable, thoughtful, and, yes, even friendly.

Before choosing a professor, Littleman recommends that students find out as much as possible about the various faculty members, and he offers the following specific points of advice:

DO NOT TAKE ANY COURSES
FROM A LIBRARY SCIENCE PROFESSOR WHO:

1. Wears a white lab coat to class because he thinks he's a scientist.

2. Does not speak English fluently unless it is a cataloging course and then it doesn't matter because you'll be asleep most of the time.

3. Wrote a doctoral dissertation entitled "The Issues Underlying the Use of Hyphens in On-Line Cataloging."

4. Claims to have been a close personal friend of Melvil Dewey and collects old catalog cards as a hobby.

5. Served on the committee that wrote *AACR2*.

6. Expects you to read anything written by the following authors: Ranganathan, Mudge, and Spofford, or published by the following publishers: Haworth, Greenwood, and the U.S. Government Printing Office.

7. Has a sign on his or her office door that says: OFFICE HOURS — 6:00 A.M. TO 6:05 A.M.

8. Gives both a midterm and final exam and takes class attendance every day.

9. Gets satisfaction out of making students cry.

10. Brags about giving out only five "A's" in 28 years of teaching.

DO TAKE A COURSE FROM A PROFESSOR WHO:

1. Uses the photography of Robert Mapplethorpe, the writings of Anaïs Nin, the pictures of Madonna, and the videos of Annie Sprinkle to illustrate the subtle differences between art, eroticism, pornography, and smut.

2. Is actively involved in an A.L.A. committee (this professor is always gone and rarely holds class).

3. Has a doctorate in something other than library science.

4. Believes that tests and grades are bureaucratic nonsense and therefore gives everyone an "A."

5. Takes thirty minute breaks during a sixty minute class.

6. Has been quoted as saying that "Cataloging is for candy-asses."

7. Holds classes in his or her home and serves everybody chocolate chip cookies.

8. Likes to be called by his or her first name.

9. Writes glowing letters of recommendation for anyone who asks.

10. Throws kegger parties at the end of the year.

What about the trend in which library students are encouraged to take some of their elective courses from other academic departments?

Dana Carlyle Shubert, a recently minted M.L.S. recipient, wrote a most interesting article on this subject entitled "What I Wish They Had Taught Me in Library School" six months after she started working as a public library reference librarian. She claims that based on her experiences every library school student should consider taking the following interdisciplinary courses:

FIVE COURSES YOU MIGHT WANT TO TAKE
TO SUPPLEMENT YOUR LIBRARY SCIENCE CLASSES

1. Self Defense 101. This will help with handling psycho patrons in the library parking lot.

2. The History of Poverty in America. Since your MLS degree is your personal ticket to poverty you really need to know something about that subject.

3. Abnormal Psychology. This could be very helpful in dealing with catalogers.

4. Pharmaceuticals 202. This will help you in being able to identify the illegal substances being sold in your library's bathroom.

5. Sales and Marketing. This will give you an understanding of how library vendors will try to sweettalk, strongarm, and swindle you into buying their products.[13]

Much has been written recently about the diverse career opportunities available to library school graduates. What are some of these options?

Yes, there have been reports from the field that recent M.L.S. holders have found jobs in such varied fields as the military, banking, computers, information brokering, public administration, securities, and communications. This however was not the experience of A. Potter Linfield, the author of a much talked-about article entitled "Parlaying My M.L.S. Into a Career as a Short Order Cook at Taco Bell." The rather sardonic Linfield bitterly complains that the options library school graduates have are much more limited than the library schools avow. What follows is his list of post degree career options:

WHAT YOU ARE QUALIFIED
TO DO WITH YOUR M.L.S.

1. Work in a library.
2. Get a job at Taco Bell.
3. Apply for food stamps.
4. Catalog your personal library using *AACR2* rules and regs.
5. Go to x-ray technology school.
6. All of the above simultaneously.[14]

Perhaps Mr. Linfield's problem was that he did not know how to com-
pose an effective résumé. What are some things that the new M.L.S.
holder should keep in mind when putting together a résumé?

The advice of library career counselor Jessica Woolley is, "Be
brief!" According to her, the biggest mistake many job seekers make is
to confuse the act of creating a résumé with the act of writing an
autobiography.

In her words, "Don't get too wordy. The idea is you want someone to read the résumé, not use it as an absorbent pad for the office
philodendron." More specifically she offers the following bits of advice:

TIPS IN WRITING RÉSUMÉS

1. Under "References" don't put any of the following names:
Jimmy or Tammy Bakker, Leona Helmsley, Mike Tyson, John Gotti,
or Ted Kennedy.

2. Under "Education" don't make a big deal of a high grade
point average. High GPA's make some employers nervous, and no
one likes a straight "A" student.

3. Under "Health" don't write: "In 1989 I was physically tor-
tured by the Russian government, and the KGB had my dentist
deliberately damage an incisor with a drill, causing a painful
abscess," even if that really did happen. Your employer doesn't
need to know this information.

4. Under "Work Experience" don't include jobs held in past
lives. Not everyone is a fruitcake.

5. Under "Why You Left Your Last Job," don't put "My boss
was an idiot." It sounds better to say, "I want to work for a more
challenging mentor."

6. Under "Hobbies" don't put "Reading about mass murderers." Someone might draw the wrong conclusion about you.

7. Under "Career Objectives" don't put "To get off food stamps." Again people will make certain undesirable inferences about you, namely that you'll demand too high a salary.

8. Under "Family Background" do not list your pets. Remember you're not applying for a job at the zoo.

9. Under "Special Talents, Skills, and Abilities" don't put down bungee jumping. Most libraries now have self-insured medical plans, therefore they don't want to take any undue risks.

10. Under "Why I Am Applying for This Job" do not put "I really like the restaurants in your community." You don't want people to question your commitment to librarianship.[15]

The résumé is only part of it. The interview is the other part. Any tips in that area?

Drew Noonan wrote the book *(Common Sense Interviewing for Librarians)* on this subject, and her approach is refreshingly down to earth. "Act yourself," she says, "unless, of course, you are a thoroughly obnoxious individual. In that case try to be someone else for an hour."[16] Among her very helpful "how not to do it" hints are the following:

TEN INTERVIEWING NO-NOs

1. Shooting wadded up pieces of paper at the interviewer's wastebasket nerf hoop.

2. Showing the scar from your recent appendectomy.

3. Wearing lip gloss (guys).

4. Wearing Doc Marten work boots (guys and gals).

5. Quoting library school professors.

6. Discussing how library school enhanced your sense of misanthropy.

7. Describing your sexual preferences.

8. Snickering when you are told the job's starting salary.

9. Asking when that "battleax who supervises the Reference Department" will be retiring."

10. Asking if the library's medical insurance plan will cover your girlfriend's breast enhancement operation?

Finally, after you've got the job, what are some things the entry level librarian should be cognizant of regarding "first day on the job" etiquette?

According to Bella Tettleton Bittmann in her article "First Day Decorum," the key is to create a nice, cooperative, low-key, "I'm not going to take over the world" impression. She says this is very important because the first day on any library job is a difficult situation. The new library school graduate is a mixed bag of conflicting emotions. There's the insecurity that goes with meeting unfamiliar people and taking on new tasks, but there's also the arrogance that comes from getting that freshly minted M.L.S.

In our rapidly changing profession there's a tendency, according to Bittmann, for new degree holders to see themselves as state-of-the-art, know-it-all, change agents. Bittmann therefore says that brand new entry level librarians should give due consideration to the following advice:

HOW TO AVOID BEING ASSASSINATED
ON YOUR FIRST DAY OF WORK

1. Do not wear a button that says, "Question Authority."

2. Do not pass out organizational charts proposing the reorganization of the library.

3. Do not put a sign on your desk saying, "THE ONLY DIFFERENCE BETWEEN THIS PLACE AND THE TITANIC IS THAT THE TITANIC HAD A BAND."

4. Do not say, "I didn't go to library school to answer stupid questions" when a patron wants to know where the bathrooms are.

5. Do not hang your library school diploma in the staff lounge.

6. Do not rearrange the furniture at the Reference Desk.

7. Do not say, "In library school we were told not to do that" when your supervisor gives a directive.

8. Do not call the library's computer "a dinosaur."

9. Do not describe the nonfiction collection as "a joke."

10. Do not refer to the director as "an idiot."[17]

Notes

1. Timothy A. Toomer, "Measuring a Job Candidate's Creativity Quotient," *Library Personnel Management Quarterly* (winter 1990) 76.

2. *Ibid.*, 77.

3. Sidney A. Bold, "The Library School Gulag," *Harper's Library Bulletin* (July 1987) 53.

4. Ridley Finn, *The Antecedents of Culture: A Unified Theory of Civilization* (London: Courtbridge Press, 1949), p. 73.

5. Andover Oppenheimer, "The Truth About the Home Computer," *Arts and Letters Review* (March 1989) 73.

6. Brookmeyer Clubbs, *The Shibboleths of Civilization: A Multicultural Approach to Human Structures, Values, and Myths* (Cambridge: Dark Friars Press, 1957), p. 1193.

7. *Ibid.*, p. 1194.

8. Stanley Bridgehopper, *The Silver Linings of History* (Hanover: A.A. Danmeyer and Co., 1989).

9. Nancy Rae Studebaker, "Geography 101: In Search of an A.L.A. Accredited Library School," *Journal of Contemporary Library Issues* (August 1992) 47.

10. *Ibid.*, 50.

11. Philip Thistlewaits, "So You Want to Be a Librarian," *The Irrepressible Librarian* (September 1992) 27.

12. Grover C. Littleman, "I Survived Library School and You Can Too," *Library Monthly* (September 1990) 71.

13. Dana Carlyle Shubert, "What I Wish They Had Taught Me in Library School," *Library Underground Newsletter* (April 28, 1991) 15–17.

14. Alfred Potter Linfield, "Parlaying My M.L.S. Into a Career as a Short Order Cook at Taco Bell," *The Irrepressible Librarian* (December 1992) 78–79.

15. Jessica Woolley, "Writing Résumés for the Right Results," *The Contemporary Librarian* (March 1989) 19–27.

16. Drew Noonan, *Common Sense Interviewing for Librarians* (Lancaster, PA: Shoofly Press, 1988), p. 73.

17. Bella Tettleton Bittmann, "First Day Decorum," *Today's Librarian* (June 1989) 18–23.

TECHNOLOGY

The computer's response time would improve dramatically if we would just stop using it to check out books.

How has technology changed the American library?

First we must understand how technology has changed America. The noted social commentator Gerald Higginbottom puts it this way: "Instead of playing baseball outside on a field with other children like I did, my ten year old son plays it alone in his bedroom on an electronic screen."[1]

What's the point?

Higginbottom's point is that modern technology's biggest impact is that it isolates us from one another. Take heating and cooling as an example. In his book *I'm a Low Tech Guy Trapped in a High Tech World,* he writes, "One winter while I was living in Wisconsin, there was a rather severe blizzard, and the electricity went out for a full thirty-six hours. Since our only source of heat was the fireplace in the living room, my wife, my son, my daughter, and I ended up spending a lot of time together huddled around that fire reading books, roasting hot dogs, and talking."[2]

This experience led Higginbottom to re-examine all aspects of his family's lifestyle, and in almost every instance he realized that technology promoted isolation rather than togetherness. For instance he noticed that instead of sitting down at one time to share a home-cooked meal, members of the Higginbottom family would drift in and out of the kitchen at random times to "nuke" a prepackaged frozen entree in the microwave oven. These informal, but substantial snacks were referred to as "whatevers" in the Higginbottom family vernacular, and eventually they took the place of formal meals. While the benefits of the "whatever" are obvious (quick, easy, everybody gets to choose what and when they will eat, and there is little or no mess to clean up), the disadvantage is also clear (lack of family togetherness). It's an important point when you remember that more than one television commentator speculated that the L.A. riots were caused by people who had never been taught the difference between right and wrong at the dinner table.

What's the point for libraries?

Quite simply that microwave oven technology is also significantly impacting the use of library staff room facilities.

Why is this important?

To understand this first we must look at some of the rather fascinating writing that Cynthia Stonestreet has done on the subject of how and when librarians talk. In her groundbreaking article "Foodspeak: A Psychogastronomic Study of Librarians," she implores us to think about all the places where real communication takes place. If we're really honest she thinks that we will admit that real talk does not happen in offices, meeting rooms, cocktail lounges, airplanes, living rooms, automobiles, and certainly not in bedrooms. "Look around you," she writes, "real talk takes place in restaurants, coffee shops, grocery stores, and kitchens. The fact is that real food produces real talk."[3]

Ellen Copplepound, in her article "The Food/Conversation Matrix: An Empirical Study Investigating Correlations Between Eating and Talking in the American Library Context," puts Stonestreet's theory to the test. What Copplepound did was analyze the relationship between food and talk in the lives of seven librarians. Her findings not only confirm Stonestreet's earlier observations but also clarify them. If you really want to know what's on a librarian's mind sit down and break bread with him or her. Copplepound theorizes that a strong causal relationship between food and talk exists for several reasons:

WHY FOOD MAKES LIBRARIANS TALK

1. Eating activates the facial muscles that librarians use to talk. This is important because many librarians are by nature very reserved and eating helps loosen up muscles that have become taut from lack of use.

2. Librarians are usually very preoccupied during the day with numerous job tasks and enjoy little opportunity for personal expression. Meals provide the needed time.

3. Hungry people are nervous people and nervous people tend to chatter rather than talk.

4. Because most staff lounges are small, people are forced to sit together while they eat. Talk flourishes when there is someone there to listen to you and respond.

5. People tend to talk about their favorite topics, and food is everybody's favorite topic.

6. Talking diverts your attention away from what you are

eating. This is important because today eating is considered a risky business. Almost every food imaginable (that actually tastes good) seems to have at least 29 health risks.

7. Talking stretches the considerable delights of eating and thereby enhances digestion.

8. Talking and eating are perfectly coordinated activities. Edwin talks while Edwina chews and Edwin chews while Edwina talks. Chewy foods obviously enhance conversation.[4]

How does microwave oven technology change the talk patterns of librarians?

According to Copplepound, the problem with the microwave oven is that it is really only effective in heating up one meal at a time. Among other things this upsets the natural talking/chewing coordination pattern. Through the use of graphs, charts, and statistics, Copplepound shows that librarians tend to eat serially rather than communally when they use a microwave oven, and she points out that this is a very important change because of how difficult it is to launch into a substantial conversation when you are just starting your meal and your companion is finishing hers. You are out of sync with one another. In our post–microwave oven staff rooms, therefore, librarians tend to isolate themselves and retreat into the private world of a book rather than take the effort to engage in meaningful communication. For Copplepound nothing could be more damaging to the psyche of the librarian. She writes, "Librarians tend to be reserved and private people who need more talk in their life. They desperately need opportunities to outwardly express their feelings of joy, frustration, anger, and ambiguity, and they also desperately need the sense of personal validation that often flows from a good, frank conversation."[5]

What other problems are created by microwave oven technology?

According to Patrick Strathmore, microwave ovens invariably increase the stress level of librarians and not just because of the negative impact they have on communication. Strathmore is the maverick library director who moved his office into the staff lunchroom because that's where he felt he could be most accessible to his librarians. In an article entitled "I May Be Fat but I Understand My Staff," he not only talks about the advantages of officing in the lounge (you're always the first to discover who's pregnant, who's getting a divorce, and whose kid got lost in the shopping mall over the weekend) but also the downsides ("it's very hard to stay away from the vending machines and you tend to feel guilty about hogging all the food that staff members bring in for everyone's enjoyment"). Perhaps the most interesting part of Strathmore's story is the ending in which he describes how he ended up moving his office out of the lounge and into the parking lot (to get closer to the patrons). "Things were not the same," writes Strathmore, "after the Friends of the Library gave the staff a new microwave oven. I had to escape the tension and bitterness that quickly ensued from the implementation of this new technology."[6]

What are the issues that library staffers have to deal with when they get a microwave oven? Strathmore identifies the following:

STAFF ISSUES CREATED
BY MICROWAVE OVEN TECHNOLOGY

1. *Who's On First?* Yes, it is true that librarians are civilized, literate, thoughtful, and unselfish, and yes, it is also true, that hungry librarians are uncivilized, thoughtless, selfish, and greedy. Getting first to the microwave oven is a very high priority if there is a possibility that you can end up sixth in line behind a circ clerk, two pages, a reference librarian, and a cataloger. Otherwise peaceful people can resort to trickery, deceit, and even threats of retaliation to get a good spot in line. Bosses routinely threaten employees with poor evaluations if they do not give them preferential treatment, and employees often leave their public service posts a few minutes early just to get a jump on everybody else.

2. *Why Can't You Eat Pizza Rolls Like Everyone Else?* Contrary to public opinion a microwave oven is not simply a "nuking" machine. Some microwave entrees actually need a bit of finesse — you know, poke a hole in the plastic covering, turn on moderate for two minutes, rotate the tray, turn on high for three minutes, remove the plastic covering, and rotate the tray 120 degrees. On the other hand there are pizza rolls — dump them on a paper plate, stick them in the microwave, turn to high, and take out after two minutes. As a result, the people who eat pizza rolls tend to get very hostile with the people who eat Chicken Oscar.

3. *Cancer Kills.* There is always one person on staff (usually a reference librarian who has read one research report too many) who considers it his true purpose in life to try to convince everybody on staff that they are going to die from microwave induced cancer. This creates a staff controversy that makes everyone very uneasy especially when someone actually is diagnosed with cancer. With most librarians, however, the lure of pizza rolls is greater than the fear of death, and all attempts to make the library a microwave free zone fail.

4. *Popcorn Kills Productivity.* There is no food known to humankind that has the drawing power of microwaved popcorn. In fact if you ever want to call a staff meeting forget about putting out a memo. All you have to do is microwave some popcorn in front of a return air vent. Everyone will come running, and that's exactly what happens every afternoon when someone microwaves a bag of popcorn for a midday snack. The trouble is there's no one left to cover the desk.

5. *Microwave Ovens Reproduce.* Eventually, and it doesn't take long, every department in the library decides it needs its own microwave oven because of all the problems that are caused by having just one microwave in the staff lounge. As a result, mini departmental staff lounges appear, and employees stop going up to the central lounge. Cliques form, and employees begin to sense a feeling, first of isolation, and then of alienation. Finally, staff morale hits an abysmal low.[7]

How about computer technology—what kind of an impact has it had upon the American library?

Actually not as significant as you might think. Consider the argument of Mustaf Hamedi as expressed in his much talked-about article, "The Engine Powered Clipper Ship." Here Hamedi compares the typical contemporary American library to a clipper ship that has been retrofitted with a diesel engine. The shape, color, form, and accommodations of the ship are exactly the same as they have been for two hundred years. The only difference is that the ship is faster and more expensive to operate. "Indeed," Hamedi writes, "most integrated library computer systems are structured to copy the form of previous manual systems. Thus, the typical computerized catalog is simply an electronic version of the old card catalog."[8]

But look at library literature, library convention exhibits, and library budget priorities. In each case computerization seems to dominate. Why is this occurring?

The reason is simple. The more we use computer technology the more dependent we become upon it. Even though people come to libraries today for basically the same reason they did 200 years ago—for books, magazines, and newspapers—we have become reliant upon the computer to catalog, index, and circulate those materials. The difference between computerized library systems and manual systems is the difference between riding a bike to work and taking the space shuttle. Sure, the shuttle is quick, but it's also expensive and complicated. Keeping it shipshape, therefore, becomes a dominant issue, and this also explains why the computer specialist has in such a short time become such a dominant figure in American librarianship. The locus of power on library staffs has consequently shifted from the administrative and budgetary functions to the technical and technological areas.

Actually to understand the impact of the library computer specialist you really should read some of the writings of Dr. E. Harold Brundage, distinguished professor of bibliographic scholarship at the Puddlesworth School of Librarianship. Brundage's main interest is in speculating on the motivations of those individuals who gravitated into computer work in the early days of on-line automation. In his highly controversial article "Library Tekkies—Who Are They and Where Did They Come From?" Brundage likens the appearance of computer specialists on the library scene to an invasion of alien beings from a distant planet. He begins the article by asking, quite seriously, "Who are these quirky, odd shaped beings who speak in clipped and cryptic tones? What planet are they from? How is it that they have so suddenly and so completely taken over control of our libraries? How has it happened that boosting megabytes is now more important than building branch libraries and that increasing computer response time is of greater importance than enhancing the book collection? Why are we more concerned with process than product, and why do we care how fast we are going when we don't even know where it is that we are going? In short who decided that the computer is God Almighty?"[9]

In answering these questions Brundage offers the speculation (based on a number of in-depth interviews with people he never identifies, for "security" reasons) that library computer tekkies are actually part of a conspiracy started many years ago by several large computer companies when their industry was still in its infancy stage. It is his view that these companies planted "moles" in libraries, schools, banks, industries, and government organizations of all types in the 50s and 60s. These moles were trained in the intricacies of computer science and were taught how computers could be used in their specific areas. They were also given specific instructions to appear wimpish almost to the point of being nonexistent. This was the origin of the computer nerd image—worn tennis shoes, baggy pants with a slide rule and later a calculator hanging from the belt, and wrinkled white shirts with the sleeves rolled up and the undershirt showing beneath the collar and a plastic pocket protector filled with mechanical pencils bulging out of the pocket.

By the middle 70s these tekkies by sheer longevity had risen unnoticed into the ranks of middle management. They now had some authority to make low level budget decisions and with that authority they began hiring consultants (who were also moles) to do automation studies showing how their company or organization could benefit from computer technology. These studies resulted in the widespread implementation of first generation computers.

According to Brundage, the mole's nose was now in the tent, and librarianship would never be the same. In the space of fifteen years, first generation computers—those slow, bulky, and undependable monstrosities—led to sleeker, more reliable but very expensive second and third generation computers, and the computer tekkie mole was suddenly transformed from an organizational oddity to a kind of technological shaman with magical powers.

In Brundage's view the tekkie's most impressive act of magic was to make the main issue of librarianship—"What is it that we should be providing our users?"—disappear, and replace it with a new priority—"*How* should we be providing services to our users?" According to Dr. Brundage, "in the span of only two decades, process has triumphed over product, bibliographic records have become more important than books, and computer tekkies have become more essential than reference librarians."[10]

Brundage's conspiracy theories, of course, have been fiercely challenged, most recently by Henriette Pennywoman, who in an article entitled "Nonsense, More Nonsense, and Damned Nonsense: A Statistical

Refutation of the Theories of Dr. E. Harold Brundage," comes to the defense of the library computer specialists, a group she describes as "quiet, dedicated, bright, and very misunderstood."[11] Pennywoman's research shows that the typical library computer specialist gravitated into computer work *after* a new computer system was installed and not before. In fact, she goes on to claim that most of the people Brundage would call "tekkies" have no formal computer training, but through hard work and "sheer fascination" have developed their knowledge and skills. In Pennywoman's words, "Library computers produced library computer tekkies. It was not the other way around."[12]

Brundage of course responded to Pennywoman's attack with an article of his own entitled "The Machine in the Library: How It Got There. Divine Intervention or Human Conspiracy?" In this refutation, Brundage hammers home the point that Pennywoman's research proves his point, not hers! He writes, "The very fact that most of the tekkies whom Pennywoman surveyed came after the computer was installed clearly indicates that the tekkies who were involved in getting that computer installed in the first place have vanished! How, in heaven's name, does Pennywoman think computers got into libraries in the very beginning? Her research should be focused on those original tekkies, not the second and third generation ones. And where are those original tekkies now? I'll tell you where they are. The giant computer companies have called these moles in from the cold and given them beachfront homes in the Cayman Islands."[13]

Regardless of which came first, the computer or the tekkie, what role does the computer specialist play in the library of today?

The computer specialist has the enormous responsibility of making sure that the library's computer system functions smoothly and cost effectively. This responsibility carries with it a great deal of stress. Catherine M. Bidwell, in her article "Coping Strategies of Library Computer Specialists," makes the point that one of the main reasons why tekkies have gotten a reputation for being weird, quirky, and off-beat is because they developed "a highly original, but sometimes misunderstood" way for dealing with situational job stress. Bidwell observes that "almost invariably computer specialists tend to anthropomorphize their computers." She is quick to add, however, that there is nothing alarming about this tendency as long as it is contained "within reasonable parameters":[14]

THE PARAMETERS OF ANTHROPOMORPHISM

1. Giving the computer a name. This is very healthy and is usually borne out of a desire for simplicity. It gets laborious to call a computer by its proper name. For instance it is perfectly understandable for a tekkie to shorten the name of a computer from HexatronAz57E to simply "Hex."

2. Giving the computer a nickname. This is a little more informal than simply shortening an official name and indicates that the tekkie is becoming more confident of his ability to understand and operate the computer. In this stage "Hex" might become "Big Guy."

3. Talking to the computer. This too is perfectly natural. Who among us when working alone doesn't talk to inanimate objects ("hey, pencil, where'd you go?") especially at night when the library is closed. It's just a normal way to cope with loneliness. In this stage the tekkie might be overheard to say something to the computer like, "Hey, Big Guy, how many books did you check out today?"

4. Identifying with the computer. In this stage the tekkie begins to make a personal identification with the computer. Now we are getting into a caution zone. A strong sense of personal identity is the key to building self-esteem and confidence. If the tekkie begins to look to the computer for personal wholeness, real identity problems can surface later on. When can you tell if a tekkie is starting to identify with the computer? Just ask the question "How are you doing?" If the tekkie says in a slow voice, "We're a little bit sluggish today — our response time is down," you might have the beginnings of a problem.

5. Falling in love with the computer. This is a definite danger zone. From an organizational standpoint having your tekkie fall in love with the library's computer is just as problematic as having your reference supervisor fall in love with one of the reference librarians. What you have to deal with is the complete lack of professional objectivity that ensues when personal relationships blossom in the work place. The tekkie loses all sense of perspective and begins throwing birthday and anniversary parties for the computer and spoiling the computer with a diverse array of expensive add-ons and enhancements. "Nothing is too good for my baby," is something you might hear the infatuated tekkie say. If your tekkie falls in love with your computer about the only thing you can do is

keep a tight rein on the budget until the romance begins to fade. It can't last forever. I mean you really have to ask yourself how long a human being can stay in love with a machine.[15]

What can be done to prevent the more extreme forms of computer anthropomorphism?

In her article "Your Computer Tekkie: An Owner's Manual," Elizabeth Simpson-Shillington offers the following three tips:

THE CARE AND MAINTENANCE
OF THE COMPUTER TEKKIE

1. *Encourage human contact.* The tekkie is definitely a person who needs people. Weird things happen to individuals who spend too much time alone. That's why it's absolutely essential to keep constant face to face contact with your tekkie even if it's just to say "hello" or "goodbye." Tekkies love to communicate by e-mail. Avoid this. E-mail is no substitute for direct conversation. It's also not a bad idea if the tekkie spends a lot of time in the computer room at night after the library is closed to call him up on the telephone once in a while just to establish that human contact.

2. *Integrate your tekkie into the library family.* All library staffs function as a kind of large extended family. Don't let your tekkie become the eccentric, flatulent uncle whom everyone tries to avoid. Make sure the tekkie attends all general staff meetings and social activities. Throw him or her a birthday party, but, by all means don't invite the computer. Finally, prohibit your tekkie from eating meals in the computer room. The camaraderie of the staff room is something that every tekkie needs to feel.

3. *Integrate your tekkie into the library's services.* Even if the tekkie does not have any formal library training, put him out on the various public service desks from time to time so that he will understand firsthand that the computer exists to support the library and that the library does not exist to support the computer. This type of experience will greatly diminish the probability of your tekkie ever saying the dreaded words, "If we just stopped checking out books, the computer would function much more quickly and efficiently."[16]

What kind of technological innovations can we expect to see in libraries in the next fifty years?

Librarian-inventor-futurist Umesh E. Dali projects that the following five technological advancements will be the most important innovations in American librarianship in the next fifty years:

1. **"Smart" Trap Doors.** The public services librarian of the future will be able to dispense with problem patrons decisively and safely simply by pushing a button and watching them disappear through trap doors located strategically in front of the librarian's service counter. These trap doors will also be wired with a built in lie detector that will activate the spring mechanism whenever a patron lies about an overdue book.

2. **"Smart" Check-Out Machines.** In the future, computers will be designed to provide custom check-out. Everyone knows that it takes a lot longer to read *Moby Dick* than *The Cat in the Hat.* The "smart circulator" will be able to determine an appropriate check-out period for each library book based upon its length, style, and subject matter.

3. **Ambulatory Book Drops.** These robotic units will be programmed to go to people's houses to collect overdue books. This will expedite circulation and cut down drastically on operational costs by making the overdue notice obsolete.

4. **Automated Catalogers.** These mechanical catalogers will not only be trained to do on-line cataloging but they will also be programmed to give you the time, the temperature, and, are you ready, a smile!

5. **Intelligence Detectors.** These devices will be able to measure the intelligence of children of all ages within the matter of a few quick minutes. These machines will be very handy when the mother of a two year old screams "My son should be in the five year old story hour! He's gifted!"[17]

What's the last word on libraries and technology?

No one can dispute that we're in the middle of a technological revolution. However, that does not mean that we should get carried away with the notion of paperless libraries and computerized home offices. Just for fun this weekend go home and watch an old Frank

Capra movie from the 30s and then watch one of the films from the Star Trek series. I think you'll find that we have a lot more in common with the past than the future. We still get up in the morning, take out the trash, and gargle with Scope. Life, when you reduce it to its basics — eating, sleeping, recreating, and reproducing — is still a rather low tech proposition.

If you don't buy that, think about all the "obsolete" forms of technology that are coming back because of the failure of new technologies to do the job. Sales of wood stoves are up and the production of nuclear generated electricity is down; the bicycle is more and more being seen as an alternative to polluting modes of transportation; and, last but not least, condoms have become the most prevalent form of birth control technology.

Twenty years ago who'd have thought it?

Notes

1. Gerald Higginbottom, *I'm a Low Tech Guy Trapped in a High Tech World* (Burlington, WI: Wood Stove Press, 1990), p. 122.

2. *Ibid.*, p. 135.

3. Cynthia Stonestreet, "Foodspeak: A Psychogastronomic Study of Librarians," *The Cutting Edge: Modern Issues for Modern Librarians* (October 1990) 88.

4. Ellen Copplepound, "The Food/Conversation Matrix: An Empirical Study Investigating Correlations Between Eating and Talking in the American Library Context," *Library Research Reports* (winter 1991) 67–89.

5. *Ibid.*, 90.

6. Patrick Strathmore, "I May Be Fat but I Understand My Staff," *The Irrepressible Librarian* (June 1992) 34.

7. *Ibid.*, 35–37.

8. Mustaf Hamedi, "The Engine Powered Clipper Ship," *Bibliotechnical Research* (fall 1988) 87.

9. Eldrich Harold Brundage, "Library Tekkies — Who Are They and Where Did They Come From?" *New Age Librarian* (November 1987) 7.

10. *Ibid.*, 15.

11. Henriette Pennywoman, "Nonsense, More Nonsense, and Damned Nonsense: A Statistical Refutation of the Theories of Dr. E. Harold Brundage," *New Age Librarian* (December 1989) 19.

12. *Ibid.*, 21.

13. Eldrich Harold Brundage, "The Machine in the Library: How It Got There. Divine Intervention or Human Conspiracy?" *New Age Librarian* (January 1991) 45.

14. Catherine Meriweather Bidwell, "Coping Strategies of Library Computer Specialists," *Library Personnel Management Quarterly* (spring 1989) 67.

15. *Ibid.*, 67–83.

16. Elizabeth Simpson-Shillington, "Your Computer Tekkie: An Owner's Manual," *Library Productivity Studies* (spring 1991) 73–81.

17. Umesh E. Dali, "Reading the Library's Crystal Ball," *New Age Librarian* (May 1993) 89–94.

SEX

When did you first realize that you needed a book on impotency?

Your column, "Facing the Public," which ran for twelve years in the Wilson Library Bulletin, *ended in the controversy of your "Librarians and Sex" survey. How did the column begin?*

"Facing the Public" also began in controversy—domestic controversy. From 1977 to 1980 I had been writing a library column for the *Burlington Standard Press,* a small town weekly newspaper published in Burlington, Wisconsin. The column, entitled "Snowballs in the Bookdrop," was my attempt to humanize the local public library by revealing many of the off-beat occurrences (the time a monkey got loose in the biographies, the time three kids brought a boat to storyhour, etc.) that make the lives of librarians more colorful than most people could possibly imagine.

I never had any intention of allowing those little weekly vignettes to find an audience outside of the friendly confines of Burlington, but my wife obviously did. "You spend all your free time writing these articles for which you receive no money," she said. "You ought to collect them together into a book. Your two children could use some new clothes, and although I know you don't care, I would prefer that our family car be a little more up to date than a '66 Rambler. Make something of your life!"

This little diatribe bothered me more than most of her little diatribes because I felt that she was laboring under three rather significant misconceptions: (1) a publisher would want to publish my homespun material, (2) I would make money on such a book, and (3) I would want to share my small town columns with a profession that was preoccupied with high technology. So I put my wife off with a million excuses, the same kind of excuses I had effectively used for not painting the house or cleaning out the rain gutters.

Finally, after a month of procrastination, she gave me an ultimatum. "Either you send your material to at least five publishers or I will never bake my meat loaf for you again." This was getting serious. There are two things in this world that I cannot do without—my mother's apple pie and my wife's meat loaf. In a fit of frustration, therefore, I composed a "query" letter to six publishers of library science books. In that letter of September 29, 1980, I resorted to the tactics of Don Rickles—to really get someone's attention you have to insult him. And so for a page and a half I challenged these publishers with insult after insult to "publish something that someone will get to at least page fifteen in." Even now I am so embarrassed by the brashness of the letter that it is painful for me to read it. At the time, however, I thought that the letter would be very effective in achieving my real goal, which was to make sure that no publisher would even consider publishing my small town articles.

Predictably and expeditiously I received nice, polite letters of rejection from Scarecrow Press, ALA, Bowker, and Libraries Unlimited. Everything was going perfectly according to plan when the unexpected happened. Two editors were actually interested. One, Virginia Matthews of Shoestring, suggested we do a book (which we did), and the other, Bruce Carrick of H.W. Wilson, suggested I might try my hand at doing some writing for the *Wilson Library Bulletin*.

Milo Nelson, who was then editor of *W.L.B.*, followed up on Carrick's suggestion, and "Facing the Public" was born. It first appeared in the January 1981 issue and ran on a monthly basis until it was abruptly terminated in June of 1992 at the command of Wilson's corporate president and owner, Leo Weins.

From the beginning, F.T.P. engendered strong reactions. The very first column, which suggested that "librarians were afraid that the mere mention of the word books would scare away users," prompted an immediate letter to the editor that claimed that I was a "questionable choice" to write this new column.

That set the tone for what was to become the monthly "point/counterpoint" aspect of the column. I would take a strong iconoclastic position on a library issue and my readers would respond in kind. Several years after I had started writing for Wilson, a woman came up to me at a state library conference where I was giving a speech and congratulated me for making *Wilson Library Bulletin*'s letters to the editor section "the most interesting reading in all of library literature." She went on to say, "I don't particularly like your column but I love to read all the letters to the editor that your column seems to generate. I'm sure Wilson hired you to create controversy."

Actually that was a misconception. The editors at Wilson always gave me the freedom to write whatever hit my fancy during a particular month, and they never specified that I be controversial. I was always capable of getting into my own hot water with no help from them. Actually, it was never my intention to create controversy. It always just sort of happened.

Maybe it had something to do with my background. I grew up in

New Jersey in a family where you were encouraged to let it all hang out. At times we took it to an extreme. Once my brother got so mad at my sister that he took a baseball bat to her face and broke her nose (or was it my sister who hit my brother with a bat?). The reaction of my mother, a Latin teacher, was to advise us to channel our points of view in a more verbal fashion. "When you really get mad," she cautioned, "it's more satisfying to pick up a pen than a baseball bat." And so I followed her advice. Instead of hitting librarians in the head with a baseball bat I wrote "Facing the Public."

You were fired from the Wilson Library Bulletin *for your survey on librarians and sex. This was deemed by the top brass at Wilson to be an inappropriate subject for a library trade journal. What was your reaction to your termination?*

I had a mixed bag of emotions. First, I thought it was totally unfair that I was made the fall guy. What about the editors? Why weren't they fired? They obviously felt that the survey was appropriate, and they made the final decision to run it. Why, therefore, weren't they held accountable? I didn't put a gun to their heads to run the survey, and I didn't break into the Wilson building late at night and sneak my survey on to their computers. Obviously, I was made a scapegoat, which didn't exactly please me in light of the fact that later, after I had been fired, I learned that reader surveys showed that I was *W.L.B.*'s most widely read columnist. So, yeah, I was bitter, real bitter.

But then when the hurt and embarrassment and bitterness of being canned began to wear off, I began to be glad I was no longer with Wilson because, hey, who wants to work for a company that should be renamed H.W. Fuddy Duddy because it thinks that sex is an inappropriate subject to question librarians about. Actually it's hard to think of another subject that is more appropriate for a survey of librarians than sex.

After all, we librarians are very defensive about our dour, sexless image. We complain about this stereotype all the time, but the problem is that we don't have any data. And that's essentially what I was trying to do—gather data. Are we in fact the prim and proper ice creatures that everyone thinks we are? Well, I was simply trying to break the ice on that very important question. That's why I used a humorous approach (Would you have sex with PeeWee Herman if he were the last man alive?), which I later found out was also considered an inappropriate way to handle such a delicate subject.

So when I was fired a lot of librarians got very indignant, not so much because they liked me but because my firing actually reinforced the stereotype of the sexless librarian. I mean what could be more maddening for librarians than to have a major library professional publication tell them that they are too delicate to be able to handle a survey on sex. What makes it even more insulting is the fact that it's hard to think of a group that hasn't been surveyed on the subject of sex. Even mainstream women's magazines like *Mademoiselle* are filled with articles and questionnaires on the "s" word, and if anyone should know that, the top brass at Wilson should know it. After all with their various periodical indexes they are the ones who give millions of Americans access to these articles and surveys.

That's why confusion was my overall reaction to getting canned. What was their motive? Had I simply outlived my usefulness as a columnist? Were they looking for a convenient reason to get rid of me? Had I been set up? Did I in fact violate their sense of good taste? Did I tread upon their higher moral sensibilities? Had I gotten enmeshed in some unseemly office politics that I knew nothing about? Had I unwittingly gotten into the middle of some long running tug-of-war between the magazine's editorial staff and the company's top management? All these questions ran through my mind, and then I finally decided that I was fired because the top brass thought that it was good business to fire me.

I had heard (via the grapevine) that management at Wilson didn't object to my column until they had gotten one or two negative letters complaining about the column's subject matter. My theory is that based upon these complaints the top brass thought that I had overstepped the bounds of what the profession thought to be in good taste. In other words, it is possible that Wilson's management was simply making the decision that they thought (based upon two letters) that a majority of librarians would want them to make. Such a miscalculation could only be based upon a stereotyped view of librarians—that we are celibate members of some weird little religious sect that worships bibliographic records, overdue fines, and silence, and that the mere mention of the word sex makes us faint.

But even worse than their complete lack of understanding about what makes librarians tick was the fact that the folks from Wilson apparently caved in to one or two complaints. What signal does this give to library boards who are faced with censors who would clamor to have books removed from library shelves? The H.W. Wilson Company's exercise of suppression is a terrible example for the library profession to follow, and it is a disheartening blow to librarians and trustees who are fighting the good and tough fight against censorship on a daily basis.

Did you feel vindicated by the many librarians and library associations that supported you after your firing?

Yes, and I do hope that the folks at the *Wilson Library Bulletin* learned from all of this that librarians are a lot more offended by the suppression of information than by articles about sex that may or may not be in good taste. Actually, where Wilson made its biggest mistake with the library profession was not so much in sacking me, but in suppressing the June 1992 issue that carried the offending column. Wilson management made the startling decision ten days after it was printed to destroy all unsold copies of the June issue and to forbid its distribution at the annual ALA conference which was held, ironically enough, in San Francisco, a city that has come to be popularly associated with a climate of sexual freedom in all its extremes.

This was a blunder. Surely these veterans of the publishing world must have realized that the best way to create interest in something is to suppress it. How could they miscalculate so badly? Again, they must have thought that what they were doing would win them a lot of friends in the library profession. Of course, all they ended up doing was elevating an obscure, little survey (that they were trying to make even more obscure) into a national story. Whenever you tell someone that you are destroying a book or magazine for moral reasons, you automatically create a tremendous curiosity about it, and the first thing people do is ask, "What can be so bad about it that it would merit burning or banning?" It's the lure of forbidden fruit that whets people's appetites for banned publications.

And that's exactly what happened with my survey. After the Wilson Company suppressed the June issue, I got hundreds of requests for copies of the survey, but invariably people were disappointed. "This is it?" they would say. "This is what the people at Wilson tried to suppress? This is what you got fired for? This isn't even up to the standards of a *Cosmopolitan* survey. I was expecting an orgy and this is a tea party. It's not even a mad tea party."

Such comments, of course, put me on the defensive. I had disappointed my defenders. No one wants to find out that they are defending oatmeal, which was what a lot of people thought about the survey once they finally got a chance to see it. In fact, after a bit of reflection, a lot of people thought that the whole episode was a publicity stunt that I had concocted to draw attention to myself and the *Wilson Library Bulletin.* "This whole thing is a hoax, right?" is the way one person put it to me. She went on to say "Wilson can't possibly be censoring this ridiculous piece of drivel except on the basis that it *is* rather dumb."

How many people actually responded to the survey?

Actually the surveys, dumb as they may be, *still* keep dribbling in. It's a rather curious phenomenon, that even now (mid-1993) over a year after it first came out and nine months after its deadline for submission, my modest questionnaire still seems to be circulating around, enjoying the celebrity status that only a censorship controversy can produce. Actually it's rather depressing to think that in five years I'll still be tabulating responses to the question, "If there were a nuclear war, and you and PeeWee Herman were the only survivors, would you have sex with him to propagate the species?"

Actually it may not be a bad idea to keep the survey going on a semipermanent basis. By keeping a running count on an on-going basis I could chart significant changes in the sexual landscape of the library profession. Wouldn't it be interesting to see, for example, what effect the aging process might have on PeeWee Herman's sexual attractiveness and his desirability to serve as the postnuclear Adam of the human race?

The downside, of course, is that I'm not all that certain that I want to be identified on a permanent basis as the library profession's Dr. Kinsey, although in all candor I could probably abandon sex surveying altogether and go discover a cure for the common cold and I'd still be referred to as the guy who got canned from Wilson for writing a "librarians and sex" questionnaire. After 43 years my identity in life seems to have been sealed.

In summary, to date (April 1993) I have received 2,797 responses to my survey.

On the basis of these responses what can you definitively say about the subject of librarians and sex?

Two things: most librarians have read *The Joy of Sex* and most women librarians have been victimized by sexual harassment by patrons. Everything else about the responses seemed rather normal and diverse or normally diverse, which I suppose means that you could draw a third conclusion—that when it comes to sex, librarians are no more easily characterized than the non-librarian population, although I must say that the fact that 8 percent of the respondees indicated that they had had an elevator sex experience seemed a bit of a surprise. I wouldn't have thought that more than 1 or 2 percent would have been experienced in this area, but then again I don't spend a lot of time around elevators because I'm afraid of them. In checking around with other people, however, I have determined that the 8 percent response level is not all that implausible in light of the fact that in the middle to late 1980s elevator sex was apparently quite fashionable. So now I always knock first before entering.

For the record here are the complete results of the survey:

1. 40 percent of the respondents felt that *Playboy* should be included in public library collections, 23 percent felt that *Playgirl* should be included, and 6 percent felt that *Playguy* should be included (12 percent commented that they did not know what *Playguy* was).

2. 61 percent of the respondents felt that public libraries should label their videotapes with G, PG, PG-13, R, NC-17, and X ratings.

3. 22 percent of the respondents felt that public libraries should check out R-rated videotapes to minors not accompanied by adults.

4. 17 percent of the respondents felt that public libraries should carry X-rated videos.

5. 22 percent of the respondents felt that public libraries should have condom dispensers in their bathrooms.

6. 14 percent of the respondents indicated that they had been sexually harassed by a library supervisor or coworker.

7. 78 percent of the female respondents and 7 percent of the male

respondents indicated that they had been sexually harassed by a library patron.

8. 20 percent of the respondents felt that sex without love is by definition bad sex.

9. 30 percent of the male respondents indicated that if there were a nuclear war and Roseanne Barr Arnold were the only woman on earth to survive, they would have sex with her in order to propagate the species.

10. 38 percent of the female respondents indicated that if PeeWee Herman were the last man on earth, they would have sex with him in order to propagate the species.

11. 6 percent of the respondents felt that AIDS is a punishment from God for those who are sexually promiscuous.

12. 82 percent of the respondents felt that Anita Hill told the truth in the Senate Judiciary Hearings, 7 percent felt that Clarence Thomas told the truth, and 11 percent felt that neither told the truth.

13. When asked to pick the Shakespearean title that best describes their first sexual encounter, 28 percent of the respondents chose *A Comedy of Errors,* 23 percent chose *A Midsummer Night's Dream,* 22 percent chose *Much Ado About Nothing,* 21 percent chose *All's Well That Ends Well,* and 6 percent chose *The Rape of Lucrece.*

14. 38 percent of the respondents classified their sex life as "romance," 31 percent classified it as "fantasy," 22 percent classified it as "comedy," and 9 percent classified it as "tragedy."

15. 49 percent of the respondents indicated that they would not pose nude in *Playboy* or *Playgirl* for all the gold in Fort Knox, 24 percent said they would do it for $1,000,000, 10 percent said they would do it for $5,000, 8 percent said they would do it for $50,000, 4 percent said they would do it for $10,000, 3 percent said they would do it for $100,000, and 2 percent said they would do it for $500,000.

16. 37 percent of the respondents lost their virginity between the ages of 19 and 21, 22 percent lost it between 16 and 18, 17 percent lost it between 22 and 25, 12 percent lost it between 12 and 15, 5 percent lost it between 26 and 30, 2 percent lost it between 31 and 35, 1 percent lost it between 36 and 100, and 4 percent claimed to still be virgins.

17a. When asked which of twelve people (Jane Fonda, Elton John, Diane Keaton, Madonna, Marla Maples, Yoko Ono, Dolly Parton, Prince, Diana Ross, Diane Sawyer, Kathleen Turner, and Tina Turner) they would most want to marry, 27 percent of the male respondents chose Kathleen Turner, 25 percent chose Jane Fonda, 14 percent chose Dolly Parton, 13 percent chose Diane Keaton, 8 percent chose Diane Sawyer, 6 percent chose Madonna, 4 percent chose Prince, 2 percent chose Elton John, and 1 percent split between Marla Maples, Yoko Ono, Diana Ross, Tina Turner, and none of the above.

17b. When asked which of those same twelve people they would most want to have sex with, 35 percent of the male respondents chose Kathleen Turner, 12 percent chose Marla Maples, 11 percent chose Diane Keaton, 10 percent chose Tina Turner, 8 percent chose Diana Ross, 7 percent chose Dolly Parton, 5 percent chose Diane Sawyer, 4 percent chose Prince, 3 percent chose Madonna, 2 percent chose Jane Fonda, 2 percent chose Elton John, and 1 percent chose Yoko Ono.

18a. When asked which of twelve people (Woody Allen, Cher, Michael Jackson, Michael Jordan, Martina Navratilova, Prince, Dan Quayle, Robert Redford, Geraldo Rivera, Arnold Schwarzenegger, Patrick Swayze, and Eddie Van Halen) they would most want to marry, 60 percent of the female respondents chose Robert Redford, 18 percent chose Patrick Swayze, 7 percent chose Woody Allen, 5 percent chose Michael Jordan, 4 percent chose Martina Navratilova, 3 percent chose Cher, 2 percent chose Eddie Van Halen, and 1 percent split between Prince, Dan Quayle, Arnold Schwarzenegger, Geraldo Rivera, and Michael Jackson.

18b. When asked which of the same twelve people they would most want to have sex with, 40 percent of the female respondents chose Patrick Swayze, 20 percent chose Robert Redford, 10 percent chose Arnold Schwarzenegger, 8 percent chose Prince, 7 percent chose Michael Jordan, 5 percent chose Martina Navratilova, 4 percent chose Woody Allen, 3 percent chose Cher, 2 percent chose Geraldo Rivera, and 1 percent split between Michael Jackson, Dan Quayle, and Eddie Van Halen.

19. 50 percent of the respondents have sex 1 to 2 times a week, 22 percent have it 3 to 4 times a week, 21 percent have it 0 times a week, 6 percent have it 5 to 7 times a week, and 1 percent has it more than 7 times a week.

20. 63 percent of the respondents have had sex in a car, 57 percent have had it in a sleazy motel room, 52 percent have had it in a sleeping bag, 43 percent have had it on the kitchen floor, 32 percent have had it in a hot tub, 20 percent have had it in a library, 7 percent have had it in an airplane, and 8 percent have had it in an elevator.

21. 30 percent of the respondents have had 2 to 5 sexual partners in their lifetime, 22 percent have had 1 partner, 17 percent have had 6 to 10 partners, 16 percent have had 11 to 20 partners, 7 percent have had 21 to 50 partners, 4 percent have had more than 50 partners, and 4 percent have had no partners.

22. When asked which of 6 things (volleyballs, gorillas, chainsaws, vacuum cleaners, yogurt, and trampolines) were an integral part of their sexual fantasies, 11 percent of the respondents checked yogurt, 6 percent checked trampolines, 2 percent checked volleyballs, and less than 1 percent checked gorillas, chainsaws, and vacuum cleaners.

23. 72 percent of the respondents indicated that they would not let a candidate's sex life influence the way that they voted in a presidential election.

24. 61 percent of the respondents have rented an X-rated movie.

25. When asked which of the following seven books they had read — *The Joy of Sex, Human Sexual Inadequacy, How to Make Love to a Man, Macho Sluts, Black Book, Unintellectual Freedoms,* and *Unprofessional Behavior* — 91 percent of the respondents checked *The Joy of Sex,* 29 percent checked *How to Make Love to a Man,* 14 percent checked *Human Sexual Inadequacy,* 11 percent checked *Unintellectual Freedoms,* 10 percent checked *Unprofessional Behavior,* 6 percent checked *Black Book,* and 3 percent checked *Macho Sluts.*

What kind of responses did you get on your optional essay question, "Describe your weirdest erotic fantasy?"

The optional essay question generated the most surprising and most critical responses on the survey. The critics berated me for using the word "weird" in conjunction with the term "erotic fantasy." Most of these people felt strongly that no fantasy should be considered weird, and that I must be some kind of a repressed neurotic cataloger for wanting to classify sexual fantasies as either "weird" or "normal."

"Even if my fantasy involved three women, two men, seven chickens, a goat, a cow, a cocker spaniel, a bowl full of goldfish, a power drill, a cherry bomb, and a Norfolk pine tree," wrote one respondent, "I would be highly offended if someone told me this was weird." Then upon further reflection, this librarian took his point even further. "Let's suppose," he continued, "that I decided to live this fantasy out. Even then you could not call it weird if the three women, two men, seven chickens, goat, cow, and cocker spaniel were all consenting participants." Having established all this, the respondent proceeded to describe in great detail his "weirdest sexual fantasy." It involved three women, two men, seven chickens, a goat, a cow, and a cocker spaniel. I thought it was weird.

Statistically speaking, 35 percent of the people who filled out the questionnaire answered the optional essay question, and most of these people did it with great attention to detail. If the fantasy involved a sunset, there was usually a very vivid description of colors, if the fantasy involved water, sometimes the respondent would give the exact temperature of the water, and if the fantasy involved an exotic location, invariably the exact degrees of longitude and latitude would be included in the narrative. This thoroughness I took as a general occupational trait. We librarians are information specialists who are trained to be as precise and accurate as possible. I almost got the feeling that many of the respondents approached the optional essay question as though it were a reference question.

But to say that the fantasy narratives were precise is not to say that they were not imaginative, lively, and wildly passionate. They were all of those things. In fact, if I hadn't promised to burn the surveys in my fireplace to protect everybody's dignity and privacy, I feel very, very confident that I could have collected them into a book entitled *The Weird Sexual Fantasies of Librarians* and made a small fortune.

Did you in fact burn the surveys in your fireplace?

Yes, everyone can rest easy. First I ran them through a shredder, then I ran over them twenty times with a pickup truck, then I sprinkled gasoline all over them, then I burned them in my fireplace. Actually I almost burned my house down. Never burn something in your fireplace that you have doused with gasoline.

How did the librarian fantasies compare to the fantasies of Madonna as expressed in her bestselling coffee table book?

Interestingly enough, the librarian fantasies were much livelier and more creative than those of Madonna. To me *Sex* was above all a depressing book. Many people said it was boring and disappointing, which I suppose is understandable given the impossibly high expectations that everyone had for it, but what struck me most about the book was that everyone in it, Madonna included, seemed so utterly unhappy. It was almost like these people were oppressed prisoners of some weird (maybe it was the austere metal cover) sexual concentration camp, a kind of pornographic Auschwitz. The whole thing made me shudder.

On the other hand, however, I couldn't be more grateful to Madonna for bringing *Sex* out when she did. For me the timing was perfect. It gave me one more opportunity to rub H.W. Wilson's nose into the absurdity of their claim that sex is an inappropriate matter to talk to librarians about. For the entire month following the publication of Madonna's opus, there was not a library director around who was not bedeviled by the *Sex* issue. Basically the question was simple: Should we cave in to public pressure and practice censorhip or should we get the book and create a terribly unpleasant public controversy that could end up hurting ourselves and our libraries? What made the dilemma even more difficult was the fact that our decision had to be made in the white hot light of media scrutiny.

What do you make of the library profession's overall response to the Madonna Sex *hype?*

For the most part, the library profession took the easy way out. Librarians tried to dismiss the whole Madonna problem as a nonissue created by media hype. Wasn't it interesting how much time was spent talking about bindings, covers, paper quality, and the threat of theft and how little time was spent talking about sex, which was what I thought the book was about? I certainly noticed this hypocrisy and grudgingly had to admit for the first time that maybe the guys at Wilson were right, librarians are uncomfortable with sex.

The other thing that librarians talked about, of course, was that there didn't seem to be any positive reviews of the book, which was not true. There were some good reviews, but they had to be hunted for in places where librarians normally do not hunt for reviews—in such obscure, alternative press publications as *Newsweek* and *The Nation.*

Why were there no good reviews in the regular library trade book review tools? This is an easy one. Several of the major book reviewing journals simply did not review the book. Their excuse was that they had not been sent review copies. For instance, *Library Journal* justified its abstinence from *Sex* by saying, "We got a chance to examine the book along with everyone else after October 21. Had we reviewed it, our review would have come out weeks after the general media reviews and too late to be useful to acquisitions librarians." So, you see, everyone had a good excuse that had nothing to do with the fact that *Sex* was about, well, sex.

The most wonderful irony of all was the twisted logic that some librarians used to justify not acquiring the book—that they didn't want to encourage censorship. Let me try to explain: if you don't get the book that's not censorship, that's selection, but if you do get the book and a bunch of patrons protest and the book gets removed from the shelf, that's censorship. So according to this logic if you get the book you're a censor and if you don't get it you're a champion of intellectual freedom.

Although librarians were very creative in manufacturing phony reasons not to get the book, I was surprised that they were not more clever. Here is my list of additional excuses that librarians could have used to justify their cowardice:

1. Patrons might get blinded by the shiny metal cover.
2. Patrons might cut their fingers on the sharp metal edges.
3. Patrons might snag their clothing on the spiral binding.
4. The book is quite heavy and if patrons dropped it on their feet they might break their little toes.
5. If the spiral binding suddenly uncoiled it could snap a patron in the eye.
6. Patrons could get eye strain trying to read the text that is superimposed over the photographs.
7. The book is too expensive to process because it does not contain C.I.P. information.
8. The book is essentially a coffee table book but if patrons put it on their coffee tables they might scratch the finish because of the sharp metal cover.
9. Because the book has a spiral binding there is no place to put a call number label.
10. Madonna is a new and unproven author.
11. The book is a mercenary scam on Madonna's part. Her sole purpose is to make money.

Actually in truth I did hear that last excuse used rather frequently by librarians, which is wonderfully comical. After all, why do Stephen King and Tom Clancy write books—to exercise their fingers?

But that's not where the hypocrisy stops. Even those brave souls who did get the book shared in the hypocrisy. I never heard anyone who ordered the book say "we decided to purchase the book because it serves a need of our users" or "we got the book because it fills a gap in our human sexuality collection." Invariably they said either "this book is a bestseller and it is our policy to satisfy popular demand" or "Madonna is an important part of our popular culture and the library is a collective memory center for popular culture." Again there was absolutely no mention of the "s" word. Even the defenders of the book, therefore, didn't defend the book's content. And they were even less imaginative in giving excuses why they did purchase the book. The list that I gave in my January 1, 1993, *Booklist* column ("Madonna, How Do I Love Thee, Let Me Count the Ways") was much more creative. Here are some of the points on that list:

1. Librarians should support authors and publishers who use extra strong covers and bindings (in this case metal).

2. The metal cover can be used as a food tray.

3. The Mylar shrinkwrap that encases the book can be used as a sandwich bag.

4. The book is dignified enough not to have a scratch and sniff feature.

5. Pet lovers will enjoy the intimate picture of Madonna with her dog.

6. This is a wonderfully appropriate way to spend the money that you saved by cancelling your subscription to the *Wilson Library Bulletin*.

7. If you keep the book shrinkwrapped and in storage, experts say that its value will double in only five years. Then you can sell it at a big profit and use the money to buy 100 paperback copies of *Moby Dick*.

8. The book will keep your library's flashers busy and out of trouble for a while.

9. There is no C.I.P. data in the book, which means that local catalogers will have an opportunity to brush up on their original cataloging skills.

10. From your circulation records of who checks out the book, you can easily determine who the perverts are in your community.

11. If enough librarians buy it, maybe Madonna will be inspired to do something nice for librarians like writing a sex advice column for the *Wilson Library Bulletin*.

12. Contrary to rumor, the book does not have a disconcerting "Where's Waldo?" feature on the page featuring Madonna and seven other people.

Now for the sixty-four thousand dollar question: did you get the book?

Absolutely not.

Why not?

Simple. I knew that if I got it, it would probably be ripped off in five minutes, and if it wasn't ripped off it would fall apart in ten minutes because of its inferior binding, and even if it didn't fall apart it would probably be taken off the shelves by hordes of angry censors. And let's not forget the fact that there were no good reviews of the book in the first place.

Actually, of course, I'm just kidding. But think of something for a minute. Doesn't every public library in the country have a collection of local church cookbooks, and aren't these cookbooks usually bound in flimsy spiral bindings, and isn't it impossible to find a positive review for any of these little cookbooks? Hmmm.

No, seriously, I have to be honest. I did not get the book for one simple reason: I considered it semi-pornographic. Okay, I admit it—that's a cop-out. The truth is I didn't think there was anything "semi" about it. To me it was pornography, pure and simple. Admittedly I am not an expert in being able to recognize the subtle nuances that distinguish eroticism, pornography, and smut, but I thought that *Sex* was definitely X rated. It's my strong impression that if the book had been written by Annie Sprinkle rather than Madonna it would have been sold in Zorba's Adult book store for ten dollars rather than in Waldenbooks for fifty.

That's not to say that pornography does not have a place in postindustrial America. Sales figures speak eloquently to that place. A lot more people are apparently buying it and renting it than just perverts and deviates. Don't forget that 61 percent of the librarians who responded to my survey admit to having rented an X rated movie. But while America has evolved both a tolerance and a taste for the stuff, it does not yet see it as the type of thing we should be spending library tax dollars on.

By not acquiring pornography aren't you practicing censorship?

Absolutely, but there's nothing new about that. We are all censors to some degree whether we are willing to admit it or not. When it comes to sexually explicit materials in the library no one's a virgin. Sure, there are some brave souls in libraryland who bought *Sex* and who subscribe to *Playboy,* but even these intellectual freedom champions cower at the prospect of venturing forth into the perilous red light district of harder core pornography. The point is that we all draw the line of censorship somewhere. Some librarians draw it further out than others, but we all draw it, and to argue otherwise is to be dishonest.

Why is censorship so rampant in a profession whose defining value is intellectual freedom?

That's because there is one value in the library profession that is even stronger than intellectual freedom: survival. If she did nothing else, Madonna proved that the survival instinct of most librarians is very well established. This is not to say, of course, that a survival instinct is bad because where would human beings be without a survival instinct? As a species, we would have been extinct a long time ago.

But is life worth living without the freedoms of the First Amendment?

That's a good point, but one that is not relevant here. By deciding not to get the Madonna book, librarians may be practicing censorship, but they are not infringing on anyone's First Amendment rights. By providing for the freedom of the press, the First Amendment guarantees Time Warner's right to publish *Sex* but does not mandate that libraries put the book in their collections.

Actually, there are some very uncomfortable tensions that exist between the First Amendment and the selection of books for the library. When you actually sit down and read the First Amendment you are startled by its simplicity. It only contains one sentence: "Congress shall make no law respecting an establishment of religion, or prohibiting the free exercise thereof; or abridging the freedom of speech or of the press; or the right of the people peaceably to assemble and to petition the Government for a redress of grievances." There are no "ifs," "ands," or "buts" to qualify the scope of the amendment. It is a law without stated limits. Madonna is free to express her wildest fantasies, and Time Warner is free to publish the results.

Library book selection, by contrast, is very limiting. That is why libraries write book selection policies—to spell out those limits. Basically there are three: money, the purpose of the library (we don't buy Danielle Steele novels for a law library), and community standards. Of these three, the third is easily the most problematic. As much as we would like to ignore the existence of community standards we can't, and what is particularly frustrating is that community standards are highly variable relative to both time and location. This makes them almost impossible to define.

In what ways are community standards relative to time and location?

What was acceptable in the post-pill sexual utopia of the 70s is now politically incorrect in our post–AIDS dystopia of the 90s. What passes as mainstream in San Francisco is considered extreme in the middle of Kansas. Not only have the rules of sexual encounters changed, but also the whole sexual landscape has been transformed into a moral war zone with heated battles being fought over gay rights, abortion, and pornography. The interesting thing is that more often than not, we librarians find ourselves in the middle of this war zone, and our vulnerability to the crossfire produced by the warring factions means that we must be quite light and shifty on our feet lest we be fatally wounded.

What is the best way to cope with the situation?

We must pick our battles carefully and then fight skillfully. Common sense helps. You don't want to get involved in a censorship battle that will give elected officials a good moral excuse to vote down library funding. It's foolhardy, for example, for a library in the Bible Belt to get the Madonna book. Not only will the book be removed from the shelf but a serious rift will probably open up between library and its community. Communities are a lot like people: you have to know how far you can stretch them before they come unglued.

But isn't defending intellectual freedom a lot like Don Quixote fighting the impossible dream? We do it even when we know we're going to get clobbered?

There is that school of thought but mostly it is espoused by people watching from the sidelines. When it comes to intellectual freedom there's a big difference between preaching and practicing, and I have found that the biggest preachers are the people who have never had to face or probably never will have to face the unfun of a nasty censorship battle.

In fact, the preachers are the ones who shame practicing librarians into lying about our deep, dark professional secret that we are all censors to one extent or another. Instead of openly admitting the fact that sometimes we have to act as censors in deference to public relations or political expediencies, we lie and tell each other that the only reason we didn't get the Madonna book was because of its flimsy binding and that our decision had nothing to do with the fact that the book is at least *semi*-pornographic.

It's sounding suspiciously like you are condoning censorship. Are you?

No, what I'm advocating is that we begin to regard intellectual freedom more as a political process and less as a religious belief. Most people, librarians included, do not make good martyrs, and yet that's exactly what our profession's intellectual freedom extremists would have us become. Martyrs. If you're the editor of a professional journal it's easy for you to exhort working librarians to spend taxpayers' money on *Sex* because you're not the one who is going to have to try to live with a disapproving city manager, an irate mayor, and an incensed citizenry.

The working librarian knows the consequences of buying *Sex*, and makes a quick decision not to get it just as a mouse makes a quick decision to scurry away from a snake. But unlike the mouse, the librarian cannot justify his action as the result of a simple survival instinct. The librarian, in order to retain his respectability as a follower of the faith of intellectual freedom, has to hide behind the shelter of a bogus excuse: "I wanted to get the book, I really did, but I just couldn't find one decent review."

An even more awkward position for the working librarian to be in, however, is the situation in which you get the Madonna book and then are forced to remove it from the shelves in response to the overwhelming protests of your patrons. In this case, there's no hiding or covering up. If you accede to these demands you're, pure and simple, a censor. The only honorable thing to do, according to the sideline cheerleaders, is to resign in protest. Again, that's easy for them to say.

Is this why librarians have such a dim view of patrons who try to pressure them into surrendering to their censorious demands?

Absolutely. Ask any librarian who the lowest cur dog in the universe is, and you won't hear any comments about mass murderers, serial killers, bloodthirsty dictators, or psychotic babysitters. Public enemy number one for a librarian is the book censor, and just as much as we hate to be stereotyped, that's how much we love to stereotype book censors.

How do we portray the average censor? If it's a man, he's a fat, balding bigot with a low, sloping forehead who wears cheap shiny suits, talks with a touch of country twang, wields a big black Bible everywhere he goes, and has some link to a weird strain of fundamentalist Christianity that teaches that all sex but procreative sex is sinful and that everyone but the members of his church is going to be damned to eternal torture. His favorite saying is "If you want to rot in Hell that's your choice," and he likes to describe in minute detail what Hell is really like. His problem with the library is that 95 percent of its books are "unGawdly."

If the censor is a woman, that's a little bit different. Outwardly she's more demure. She looks like a cross between Phyllis Schlafly and the 1950s version of Betty Crocker. The ankle length dresses, the gold cross around the neck, and the bulky, flat soled shoes are the giveaway. This person talks more about the evils of secular humanism than the tortures of Hell. She appears to mean well, but comes across as an unschooled, naive captive of some intolerant and manipulative preacher. She may seem harmless, but she's actually quite unrelenting when it comes to badgering board members and organizing political pressure on city councils. She is the type of person who chains herself to the front doors of an abortion clinic. She is the most difficult of censors to vanquish.

These unpleasant caricatures stem from our absolute opposition to censorship in all of its forms. We believe that as librarians we should have absolute freedom to choose whatever books and magazines that we want for our libraries. We feel strongly that this is a right that is guaranteed to us under the First Amendment of the Constitution. We truly believe that the library should be the one place in our communities where all points of view and all forms of expression are tolerated, collected, cataloged and made available to anyone who wants access to them for whatever reason. We, therefore, naturally resent anyone who would attempt to infringe, curtail, or limit us in our pursuit of this goal. In short, we have no tolerance for the intolerant. Those who would practice censorship are as odious to us as the practice itself.

But isn't there an uncomfortable irony in our attitude?

Unfortunately, yes. The irony, of course, is that our own intolerance for censors constitutes a form of censorship. How often at our professional meetings, seminars, and conferences do we invite and listen to the censor's point of view? How often have the Jerry Falwells, Phyllis Schlaflys, Pat Buchanans, and Dan Quayles of the world been invited to speak at ALA intellectual freedom programs and seminars? The answer, of course, is not very often. We prefer to have our own positions and perspectives validated rather than challenged. We are the biggest defenders of intellectual freedom except when it comes to the subject of intellectual freedom itself. Then we become close minded.

The further irony is that censors are essentially people who vigorously exercise their own intellectual freedom rights. Take a second, closer look at the text of the First Amendment. Here's what it says:

"Congress shall make no law respecting an establishment of religion, or prohibiting the free exercise thereof; or abridging the freedom of speech or of the press; or the right of the people peaceably to assemble and to petition the Government for a redress of grievances."

By showing up at library board meetings, therefore, and raising holy Hell about the library's acquisition of Madonna's latest book, the censor is merely exercising his Constitutional right to petition a government body. By ridiculing the censor as an intolerant bigot, therefore, we are simply displaying our own pathetic lack of understanding of the First Amendment, and this lack of understanding reflects badly upon us.

Too often in our local censorship battles we come off as elitist, peevish, and arrogant. We hear what the censor is saying, but we don't really listen to his arguments because we assume inherently that he has discredited himself by the very act of requesting that certain books be taken off the shelf. The irony, however, is that because we don't really listen to him, we don't effectively refute his points, and more often than not we consequently lose the argument. The censor ends up petitioning the government and winning, and in our defeat we become even more elitist and arrogant when we complain about self-righteous censors and the cowardly political officials who cave into their intolerant demands.

There's a lesson here: intellectual freedom is an uncontrollable beast that can be turned against us. We make a huge mistake when we think that the beast will always be used for the "right" things. Intellectual freedom is actually the reason why democracy is so messy and at times unseemly. It protects the pornographer as well as the preacher, the reactionary as well as the radical, and the sinner as well as the saint. Even the people we dislike have a right to their intellectual freedom and that oddly enough includes those who would use that freedom to censor others.

Okay, so if we can't simply censor censors how do we handle them?

Just because censors have a right to speak their mind doesn't mean that we have to coddle them even if they are sincerely concerned about things like community values and individual morality. If dismissing them out of hand is both unfair and ineffective, then obviously the opposite strategy is the one that we should use. We must force them to be as specific and as detailed as possible and then we must listen to their specifics and refute them cogently point by point. The best way to disarm a censor is to pin him or her down.

How exactly should you go about doing this?

In many respects we librarians need to think and to act like attorneys conducting a cross examination. Let the censor have his say and then play twenty questions with him:

TWENTY QUESTIONS MOST CENSORS DO NOT WANT YOU TO ASK THEM

1. You say this book is immoral. Please explain to the Board (or the City Council) exactly what you mean by that?

2. How do you define the word "immoral"?

3. Do you think that everyone who lives in this community would define "immoral" in that way?

4. Do you think that everyone who pays taxes in this community to support the library shares your moral values and ethical beliefs?

5. Do you feel that you have a right to impose your concept of morality on the other people who live in this community?

6. What exactly in this book do you consider to be immoral?

7. Can't you be more specific? Please give us a listing of the pages and passages that you find morally objectionable.

8. What exactly is it about those pages and passages that you deem to be harmful?

9. Specifically what harm do you think would result if someone read those pages and passages?

10. Do you have any research-based data that would support your claim that these pages and passages could have a harmful effect on our citizens and our community?

11. Can you cite any published book reviews that would support your claims and positions?

12. Have you read the professional reviews that recommend this book for inclusion in library collections?

13. Why should the library board accept your perspective over the recommendations of those who review books for a living?

14. Is the library forcing anyone to read this book?

15. Shouldn't people be allowed to decide for themselves whether or not they want to read this book?

16. There are people in this community who have requested this book. What gives you the right to deny them their right to have access to this book?

17. How would you feel if someone censored a book that you wanted to read because they said it was harmful, immoral, or unethical?

18. In a democratic society shouldn't each individual have a right to have access to all points of view and all forms of expression?

19. Do you think that most of your fellow citizens are incapable of deciding for themselves what they and their children should and should not be reading?

20. What do you think would happen to the library if the board took a book off the shelves everytime someone objected to it on the basis of his or her own personal morality?

By asking all these questions aren't you going to antagonize the censor and exacerbate an already volatile situation?

Absolutely not. My game of "twenty questions" is meant to inform and educate the censor rather than to harass and antagonize him. The fact of the matter is that most censors really are sincere. They really are trying to do what they think is right for the library's community. They either see themselves as concerned taxpayers who do not want public monies spent in inappropriate ways or as concerned community leaders who do not want the library to be a corruptive influence especially for young people.

The real intent of the questioning exercise, therefore, is to give them something to think about rather than their own moral values. Most censors have not thought out the ramifications of what they are trying to do because they simply do not understand what role a library plays in a democratic society that protects individual rights of expression.

The key concept that we want to get across to censors is that if they have the right to take books out of people's hands, then other people have the right to take books out of their hands. The twenty questions are intended to show the censor that he who lives by the sword of censorship can sooner or later die by it.

Notes

1. Will Manley, "Madonna, How Do I Love Thee, Let Me Count the Ways," *Booklist* (January 1, 1993) 773. Additional reasons given to get Madonna's new book: "Madonna defended the Pope against the attacks of Sinead O'Connor, and we have to assume that some of the profits from the book will be used to support the Vatican's Third World poverty programs; there is a free compact disc with every book; and the book can be useful to children's librarians who are in the habit of reading picture books to their spouses at bedtime."

APPENDIX

The Doctor is performing an appendix removal.

Please send this questionnaire to:
Will Manley
P.O. Box 23665
Tempe, AZ 85285-3665

1. Put a check by what you think is the best use for this book.
   ☐ Firewood kindling
   ☐ Hot plate pad
   ☐ Window prop
   ☐ Hot air balloon ballast
   ☐ Something to read
   ☐ Other _____

2. Put a check by the place where you read most of this book.
   ☐ Office
   ☐ Staff lounge
   ☐ Reference desk
   ☐ Traffic signals and railroad crossings
   ☐ Bed
   ☐ Easy chair
   ☐ During TV commercials
   ☐ Bathroom
   ☐ Other _____

3. Put a check by the one word that best describes this book.
   ☐ Terrible
   ☐ Pretentious
   ☐ Mediocre
   ☐ Average
   ☐ Okay
   ☐ Enjoyable
   ☐ Informative
   ☐ Other _____

4. If you were an original cataloger what subject heading(s) would you use for this book?

_____

_____

5. Is this book worth the $21.95 that you paid for it?
☐ Yes
☐ No

6. Which chapters did you enjoy most and least?
Most _____
Least _____

7. If you could take either this book or Madonna's book to a desert island which would you take?
☐ *The Manley Art of Librarianship*
☐ *Sex* by Madonna

8. After reading this book would you be inclined to read another book by me?
☐ Yes
☐ No

9. What advice or suggestions do you have for me for future books?
_____
_____
_____
_____
_____

INDEX